Change to Li

D1151329

Change to Life

The Pastoral Care of the Newly Retired

Roger Grainger

> *Age is opportunity no less*
> *Than youth itself, though in another dress . . .*
> *H.W. Longfellow*

DARTON · LONGMAN + TODD

First published in 1993 by
Darton, Longman and Todd Ltd
1 Spencer Court
140–142 Wandsworth High Street
London SW18 4JJ

ISBN 0–232–52033–X

A catalogue record for this book is
available from the British Library

Phototypeset by Intype, London
Printed and bound in Great Britain
at the University Press, Cambridge

For Doreen,
with love

Contents

Acknowledgements

I should like to thank everyone who responded to my SOS in the *Church Times*, and others who have given me help and advice. In particular, I should like to acknowledge a very real debt to the following: Doreen Grainger, Michael Grainger, Joan Sygrove, Malcolm Aldcroft, Bee Kenchington, the organizers of the 1991 Wakefield Diocesan Clergy Retirement Conference, and Anne Aliffe, for her patience and professionalism.

Introduction

Retired people play a more noticeable part in society now-adays than they ever did before. They dominate voluntary associations and church organizations. They crowd the meeting halls and places of entertainment deserted by those who are working or looking for work. They provide a ready market for commercial exploitation, ranging from 'holidays for the over-sixties' to the explosion in private residential care. More and more attention is paid to the political power of older people, particularly with regard to their ability to influence decisions about the allocation of resources for health and social welfare. 'Far from being the object of other people's charity,' says Magnus Pyke, 'elderly people can play a decisive part in shaping their own destiny, one which affects the nature of society itself.'

There has been a marked rise in the numbers of retired people since 1945. In 1951, 87.7 per cent of men aged 60–64 were still at work; by 1968, it was 53.4 per cent. During the same period opportunities for working after the state retirement age (currently 65 for men, 60 for women) rapidly diminished; in 1951, 20 per cent of men who were older than 70 were working or registered as seeking work, but by 1968 the figure had dropped to below 5 per cent. Early retirement has also grown rapidly; by the early 1990s it is estimated by some that half the men in the 55–59 age group had left the labour force. The trends for women are similar, except for married women aged 55–59, who have become more economically active, rising from 48 per cent in 1973 to 52 per cent in 1983. Increased life expectancy during this century has caused the number

1

of people of retirement age in Britain to increase from 2.2 million in 1901 to 9.7 million in 1981.

Retirement, then, is a tremendously important social factor. Large groups of people find their lives changed because of it. Some of the most important ways in which this can happen will be described in this book. I shall be concentrating on personal emotional experience rather than social behaviour, although both these things are powerfully affected by changes in how much work we have to do and what we are paid for doing it (or not doing it!). This is a book about how it feels to be a retired person. However 'sociologically significant' retirement may be, there are good reasons why it is a testing time emotionally.

Retirement has been described as the life event which marks the beginning of old age. Old age is not very popular; it has what people nowadays refer to as a negative image and, because of this association of ideas, there is a tendency to regard retirement negatively as well. In fact, retired people tend to show considerably more contentment than society as a whole shows. A study carried out in 1977 by Age Concern revealed higher levels of 'life satisfaction' among the retired than was the case among younger age groups. Younger people, even though they had, as a rule, more money to live on, were far less contented and had a greater sense of being deprived of the happiness they would have had if they had had more money to spend on holidays, deep-freezers, washing-machines and spin-driers, more prestigious housing and faster, more luxurious cars. Obviously, quite a few of us become happier as we get older! At the same time, the change from productive middle age to retired elderly status is a dramatic one, and requires a considerable degree of adjustment. Accommodation to a different set of life circumstances may take from several months to many years. Some people, because of the circumstances in which the event takes place, which are different for everybody, and their own special life history and personality structure, may need specialized help. Others are dependent on the understanding and compassion that

other people can give them. Loneliness, depression, a
sense of having lost all purpose in living are quite normal
reactions to having to relinquish the job that they have
held for many years; to which they owe their sense of
'being someone', someone with a socially valued role,
performing a task really well, as only they know how to
do it, because they have done it so long, and because they
know how important it is. This kind of distress may be
temporarily relieved with the help of psychiatric medi-
cines; it can only be brought to a really positive outcome
by being lived through with a degree of awareness of
what is taking place. For this there is no substitute for
friendship. Friends are the people who do not leave you
alone, but go along with you, thus demonstrating that
you are going *somewhere*. Psychologists point out that the
two factors associated with retirement that are responsible
for most of the episodes of real illness occurring at this
time are diminished self-esteem and difficulties in personal relationships. The two things belong together, each
contributing to the other. It is a great pity when retirement
is not only regarded as an unnatural event but when, in
addition, the symptoms of major life change are inter-
preted in wholly psychiatric terms, as if they were signs
of mental illness. On the other hand, to pass retirement
over with a stiff upper lip, as if it involved little or no
real psychological stress, is certainly just as bad. People
making this voyage need to know more or less where the
storms are likely to break. So do their friends.

In a book written some years ago, Magnus Pyke wrote
that

> Life is a continual process of change. To a philosophical mind,
> it is a fruitless task to try to rank its various stages in order of
> their agreeability, or importance, or usefulness. Happiness can
> come at any age. Heroic deeds that illuminate human history
> can be done by old men and women as well as by young ones.
> Christ made his contribution and died in his thirties. Pope John
> set a standard for Christianity in his eighties.

Amen to that!

1. When, How and Why? From and to What?

Retirement as we know it today is a comparatively recent thing, the product of what the great nineteenth-century French sociologist Durkheim called 'the division of labour'. This signified the emergence, under the pressure of an industrialized society, of precise systems of rules as to how the complicated workload should be apportioned – who should do what, and when, and for how long. Before this, a man or woman would simply carry on working until old age or sickness forced them to hand over to a successor, who would move up the occupational ladder and take their place. More kinds of jobs demanded more workers, which meant, in turn, a greater turnover. Specialization involved more trades, more workers, a greater workflow. At some point in their life, people must be made to stop working.

A lot of people, of course, are only too glad of the excuse. In more than one sense of the word, work may be unrewarding: strenuous, boring, socially undervalued, poorly paid. For one reason or another a job which used to be a source of satisfaction and pride may become wearisome, so that the woman or man who goes on doing it begins to feel stale and devalued along with the job. Someone may have developed interests or hobbies which, over the years, have begun to usurp the place in their lives that their job once held. Perhaps they have a particular project put by for retirement, something they can't wait to get down to; or perhaps they feel that they have simply done enough. The task is finished, the race has been run, the hour is struck, and it is time to down tools. Such people are probably more numerous than one may think. It may be, in fact, that they are in the majority.

This book is not about people like them. I am tempted to say that those who enjoy this kind of well-deserved rest from their life's work hardly need to have a book written about their pastoral care. However, it is not quite as simple as that. Change of any kind that affects the way in which we see ourselves (and consequently feel about ourselves) is likely to have a disturbing effect upon our general ability to cope with day-to-day living, and this is true whether the change is a welcome one or not. Certainly, it helps to prepare for such things in advance, but the trouble is that we tend to confuse preparation with rationalization; we learn ways of thinking round the idea of change so that we come to believe that we have already got used to the difference before it has happened. We do this with both 'good' changes and 'bad' ones; it is the fact of change itself that we are trying to avoid, and whose effects we are trying to forestall. We shall be looking at this again later on. For the moment, however, it is worth pointing out that people who claim to have had no difficulty at all in adjusting to retirement may be among those most profoundly affected by it. As with bereavement, 'taking it well' may mean precisely the opposite.

This book, then, is about helping people to cope with the emotional effects of a particular kind of change, the kind involved in becoming retired from doing a particular job for a number of years. This is an event of some significance, something to be taken seriously. In some cases help is required in getting adjusted to a new situation, one which requires the person concerned to learn how to do new things in a new way, and not to do old ones any more in any way at all. In so far as our sense of identity depends on our mental view of ourselves 'in action', the new state of affairs requires a new sense of self. Perhaps a new job could supply this, bringing with it new aims, new skills, new contacts. For many retired people, however, this is not possible. Whatever is done to assist must be done in terms of aims, skills and contacts which already exist, having survived the upheaval.

By far the most important of these are the contacts. Contacts with other people play a vital part for those going through major changes in the way their lives are organized. Of the factors which go to make up our picture of the world, other people are by far the most important. People and events are closely intertwined in our experience of life: we get up at a certain time, have breakfast at the same time each day, catch the same bus, walk to work along the same street, and every day we come into contact with the same people, some of whom we know personally, some we don't, but all of whom we recognize. Once we get to work, things get even more familiar, more personal. Whether or not we actually enjoy our job, while we are engaged in it we are in a sense supported by it, held in the network of interrelated roles which constitutes our working life. At the time it may feel to us as though this network of interactive relationships is a painful restriction of individual liberty, that we are in fact trapped by the work we do and kept in place by the presence of so many other people actively engaged in doing things which, however diversified, are all basically similar, all part of the universal business of earning a living.

Once these links are broken, the world can look very different. Perhaps there are other networks – friends and neighbours, people whose interests and hobbies one shares – which can be developed to take the place of the working world which has been used, and taken for granted, for so long. Networks of this kind fulfil an essential purpose in allowing us to be human. At the same time they reflect our individuality by providing a foil to our own personal lives, and build up a sense of solidarity with other members of the race. I shall argue in this book that, whether we are solitary or gregarious, introvert or extrovert, we depend on networks of other people in order to maintain our basic humanity. These 'personal identity plans' may represent people who are present or absent; the essential thing is that they should *exist*.

Support networks can, of course, be provided. If we want to help those who are suffering a disruption of their lifestyle, a dramatic twist in their personal story (and retirement is very often this, even when it is not acknowledged to be so), we must be willing to work towards helping them to spin a new web of relationships, either openly or secretly according to personality and temperament, to replace the kind of 'background belonging' involved in their experience as employed persons – the feeling of being a contributing member of the community, part of the social fabric. In other words, if we want to help them we must find a way of restoring their impaired sense of helping us – or, at least, of playing a part in the system which supports us all, the continuing life of the world. Nowadays, this feeling of global interdependence is more powerful than ever before. It has always been a basic part of Christian teaching, of course. With the heightened sense of our own personal involvement in the welfare of the entire planet have come more opportunities for us to feel that we can do something, however small, to help. This is useful work, more useful than many of the things we are accustomed to being paid for doing. It can be useful enough to repair some of the damage to our sense of belonging caused by retirement.

On a more circumscribed, but no less personal, level the local church may, and very often does, play an important part in re-socializing the recently unemployed by bringing home to them their community identity. Every Sunday, and sometimes during the week as well, they are surrounded by people who appreciate their individuality and remember their actions within a shared history. It seems to be the case that congregational life largely depends for loyalty and enthusiasm on two groups of people: those who are too young to be in full-time employment, and those who are old enough to have retired from it. These are the people who put most into and consequently receive most from church membership. They form a more or less permanent focus of identity, the Christian in the church, the church in the neighbourhood, throughout the country, and into the world, an expanding circle of implicit personal belonging, depending at the centre on face-to-face relationships within the 'spirit-filled community' of the local church. Granted, this kind of thing is often said, and even more often preached; but it is precisely such an expanded universe of belonging – the suggestion that my own individuality is securely enmeshed in the fabric of human corporate existence, so that what I say has *implications* – that I am in danger of losing once I surrender my place in the real world of those who earn their living. Certainly, there is an important difference between these two kinds of belonging: the difference between things that are earned and those that are received freely, as a gift, and this is something else which must be looked at in this book. There is, however, a sense in which belonging is belonging, whatever the circumstances. Even if we would perhaps prefer to earn, we are nevertheless happy to receive, so long as we can feel genuinely involved.

Making people feel involved is, in fact, the great practical challenge confronting the local church. Some local churches are better at it than others. There is no doubt, however, that it should be a priority for every congregation. It is, after all, what congregation means. On the other hand, this certainly does not mean that churches exist in order to provide people with jobs, paid or otherwise – there is certainly very little that I can find in the Old or New Testaments about that! There is, however, a good deal that says very clearly that human gifts should be used creatively in God's service – see, for example, the Parable of the Talents (Matthew 25:14–29) – and that the Christian Church itself is essentially an environment in which individual men, women and children should find the kind of employment ideally suited to their own unique talent and personality:

> For indeed we were all brought into one body by baptism. . . . A body is not a single organ, but many. . . . God appointed each limb and organ to its own place in the body, as he chose.

9

> If the whole were one single organ, there would not be a body at all; in fact, however, there are many different organs, but one body. (1 Corinthians 12: 13, 14, 19, 20)

Unfortunately, it is only too easy to interpret St Paul's words in a *spiritualizing*, rather than a genuinely spiritual, sense: in other words, to treat them as though they referred to particular dispositions of social or spiritual abilities rather than real actions in the real world. Paul intends something much more direct, much more in line with Jewish theological tradition, than this. The body of Christ is constituted from entire persons, who are its organs: a wholeness of wholenesses. It is people with gifts, gifted people, who are being referred to here and elsewhere in the Epistles. We are so used to having to pass examinations to establish the fact that we have learned enough, and IQ tests to discover if we are clever enough to start learning at all, that we impose own world-view on Paul, and wonder what job we are qualified to aspire to! Are any of us apostles, or prophets, or teachers, or miracle workers? Is there a healer in the house? As for tongues . . .

There is a moral here for congregations who want to attract new members. So many times church councils get their heads together and try to make the church richer and more efficient by 'attracting new skills' into the fellowship, to bring it into line with modern management techniques perhaps, or simply to improve the standard of organ-playing or choral singing. The decision is to ask Mr So-and-so who is a specialist in whatever it is that is wanted, having recently retired from doing it professionally. Mr So-and-so is gratified when the vicar and a member of the PCC call on him in order to ask his help. It may be that he hasn't been to church for a long time, and wasn't really thinking about going again. Perhaps he used to go when his wife was alive, but now spends Sunday mornings gardening and thanking God that he can finally do what he wants when he wants. He should have retired earlier instead of waiting until he was heartily sick of the place. . . . Nevertheless, he feels flattered that the church wants his help, and says he'll definitely think about it. When the vicar implies that the whole thing is on the verge of collapse unless he, Mr So-and-so, steps in and saves it, he capitulates – 'Yes, I'll renew my membership. . . . Only too glad to.'

He doesn't stay very long, however. There is much more to belonging than performing a particular task. If he doesn't feel he belongs in church, the morning service comes a poor second to a spot of quiet gardening. It may be a long time before his particular skill is needed, and by then somebody has probably emerged from the congregation itself, someone more deeply embedded in church life than he can ever be, a *real* churchperson.

Unfortunately, the vicar and his helpers had got things the wrong way round, going for the skill instead of the person. Certainly people like, or even need, to feel useful. The great gift the church has to bestow is that of making people feel *valuable*. This, above all, is what membership of the Body of Christ means; to take part in Christ means to share something, or someone, of inestimable value. It is primarily you whom this concerns, and only secondarily your gifts. Indeed, your gifts are called forth by membership, as expressions of the corporate self-awareness involved in the experience of belonging. Durkheim called this the 'conscience collective'. It is able to give strength and comfort to people who believe they have no gifts at all, certainly none that can be realized in terms of cash value or organizational efficiency. It is probably true that every religious community possesses this characteristic, which is a kind of baseline religious belonging. Church members know very well that 'the wind blows where it wills' – or at least it does so for *them*. Either they will set forth in precise detail why it is that they prefer one congregation to another, or they will say that they simply do, and can't say why.

At any rate we recognize the Holy Spirit when we encounter it, and we find ourselves drawn into the fellowship bringing our gifts with us. It is not as automatic and

11

impersonal as this, of course. The Holy Spirit is never either of these things. Congregations can work hard to make themselves more friendly and welcoming, more 'genuinely Christian'. We all know that there is very convincing evidence that the Spirit does come when it is called, and that our hearts are inspired. The point I am making is that we should set about doing this first, so that we can really provide a lively welcome for those who need our support and encouragement, rather than confronting them with a collection of individuals who, if you asked them to be frank to you, would probably admit that they were bored with the church and resentful of one another. If things are as bad as this, or if it looks as though they might get as bad, it is really not fair to expect a stranger to put them right. Pretty soon he or she is likely to wonder about the real reason for the invitation, which appears to involve a good deal more than the skills they were trained for.

Retired people, then, should be invited into the congregation in the first place for their own sake. At this time in their lives they may well need the support and encouragement that the church can give. It is important that they should feel welcome for themselves and not simply because they may be useful. If they are helped to settle in first there is a good chance that they will help build up the Body of Christ in ways that neither the congregation, nor they themselves, had ever expected. Psychologists who have studied creativity have demonstrated that this is in fact the way these things happen; in other words, the times when we think in the most original and positive way are preceded by periods of comparative quietness and relaxation from stress when we abandon our habitual preoccupations and let our thoughts move in any direction they choose, so long as it is away from anything connected with the purposeful solution of problems. George Kelly refers to a process of 'loosening' followed by one of 'tightening'; ideas that have presented themselves during the first phase are specifically related to the task in hand during the second. The result resembles Edward de Bono's

12

'lateral thinking', according to which problems are solved by being approached from previously unconsidered angles.

It may well be that what a newly retired person needs as much as anything else is precisely this – an opportunity to 'creep up on life'. One set of reins has been laid down; there is no urgency on his or her part to take up another set and go rushing away down a fresh path, particularly if it turns out to be the same, in disguise. Generally speaking, what a retired person needs at this juncture of her or his life is the church at its most nurturing and supportive. Whether or not a newly retired person is a new member of the congregation, or an already established one, it is probably better to think in terms of their starting afresh along an entirely new path rather than simply employing old skills in a new setting. If retirement is about a significant psychosocial change, something that affects the lives of individuals and community, surely it provides an opportunity for new beginnings; and if this is the case, a good deal of care must be taken simply not to get in the way of whatever it is that is emerging. It would be a brave congregation that was willing to take this principle to its logical conclusion by allowing someone to sever their links with the church if they felt moved to do so. All the same, if we are to play the role of midwife to significant changes in people's lives (and I can't think of any agency more suited to the task) we must have the courage of our convictions and perform it in love, not selfishly and for our own gain.

It would be a very great pity to lose such a source of creativity, however, and one would search diligently for alienating factors within the congregation which might have led to the decision to leave. On the other hand, if church membership was closely associated with, or dependent upon, the lifestyle involved in a particular social position, then once that position can no longer be sustained, through lack of funds, in the way that it formerly was, membership of the congregation may appear to have lost some of the benefits it once had. An example would

13

be the case of a retired member of one of the less-well-paid professions who, prior to retirement, enjoyed church for social as well as religious reasons, seeing it as a pleasant and useful way of 'keeping in' with clients and their families, but now finds it necessary for financial reasons to narrow the scope of his or her social life and to come less often to church. This may seem a reprehensible use of the church for selfish ends, but a moment's reflection should remind us of times when it has been so much easier for us to stay at home than run the risk of meeting somebody we would prefer not to – not just at the moment, at any rate. Our reasons for going to church tend very often to be mixed, and sometimes it is the least spiritual one that comes out on top.

I realize that the use of the word 'creative' may startle people who are accustomed to seeing it used to mean artistic in the narrow sense. I am not suggesting that retired people fill in their time by learning to paint or draw or produce fine needlework. This would certainly be the right thing for some; equally certainly, it would not suit everybody. Many people can remember from their schooldays the discomfort caused by having to be 'artistic': it was worse for us than for the people who were forced to find words for our drawings and be tactful about our violin-playing. I use the word 'creative' in this context to mean 'an original way of behaving which serves a worthwhile purpose'. Creative behaviour often seems to result from combining ideas and perceptions which were previously unconnected, or not connected in that particular way. When patterns of behaviour and ways of making sense of things have been disrupted, when we no longer have any idea what to expect from life and feel completely disorientated, then any response which brings a sense of purpose and a feeling of hope creates new life for the future. Where the pattern of life is broken, any healing is creative.

The Church is a healing community – this is the aspect of Christianity involved in the pastoral care of those who have recently retired. If, during the first few years of

14

retirement, a person feels understood and valued by other people, he or she stands a better chance of adjusting to the conditions imposed by a new way of living than they would if such support had not been forthcoming. This book has been written to assist would-be helpers to understand some of the factors involved in the experience of retirement. Understanding is very important. It is this, I believe, that helps wounded people to heal. Throughout the book I shall suggest various ways in which particular states of mind may be either established or discouraged. Most of the time, people find the weeks and months leading up to and following retirement a time of emotional unrest; they may doubt their ability to come to terms with the new situation, they may already be grieving for the way of life which must soon be abandoned. Their unhappiness and restlessness affects the people with whom they live and work, so that rows become more frequent or start happening where relationships were formerly calm and equable. The expectation of personal and social change may prove more difficult to live with than the changes themselves when they actually arrive. Crisis throws its shadow before itself: psychological investigations show that more disturbance occurs during the last months before retirement than in the time following the event, and actually including it. Bromley has shown that 'it appeared that the critical period for adjustment might not be retirement itself but the period just before retirement', and that during this time people 'become increasingly agitated about its consequences and problems'.

In a way this is not surprising. I can think of two reasons why there should be more open distress before than after retirement. The first of them is social. It is definitely more acceptable to resist oncoming retirement than complain about its arrival. The desire to go on working in the same way for as long as possible is, as we shall see, a dominant social virtue, as is the willingness to accept whatever has already happened with stoical resignation. Both contribute to a feeling of stability within the community. Psychologically, this way of reacting makes sense in terms of a

often physical symptoms occur due to adrenalin!

resistance to changing behaviour patterns which are well established and systematically reinforced, and the funda-mental human need to 'make the best of a bad job'. This is Festinger's celebrated explanation for behaviour caused by 'cognitive dissonance': that the simultaneous presence of two conflicting ideas leads to an insupportable mental state that motivates the person concerned to reduce the 'dissonance' between them. In this case the best way of coping with the fact that retirement is there, and won't go away, is to stop loathing it and start loving it instead. In other words, we convince ourselves that there is simply no problem at all.

However, the purpose will be to explore various ideas in order to gain a greater understanding of what it is like to be someone who has recently retired and has not come to terms with it yet. This means that I shall approach the subject from several angles, hoping to build up a picture which readers will find recognizable, either in their own or other people's experience. I have no doubt that different parts of the book will strike a chord with different people. It is not all immediately applicable to every retired person. For instance, it is obvious that somebody who has been preparing for retirement for years, looking foward to it with eagerness and making definite plans about how they will occupy the increase in leisure time involved, will experience the event when it arrives quite differently from a person who is suddenly made redundant when he or she believed that a few more years of productive labour lay ahead of them. For the second there will be feelings of shock and intense disappoinment, grief even, that the first will almost certainly be spared. Retirement is some-thing that is more or less painful, more or less disruptive. I am concerned here as to how we can help people who are finding it traumatic, whose lives have been transformed by its onset. It may well be that the vast majority of people are not affected in this way, and there is no point in writing about them. Certainly there is nothing Christian about making people needlessly anxious. If I am concerned with something that only happens to a few people, I have no right to present it as if it were of general concern.

In fact, however, this is not the case. Wherever there is a change of this magnitude, involving the reversal of long-standing habits and the abandonment of well-thought-out and firmly entrenched practices – the rebuilding, in fact, of an individual human life in all its interior dispositions and exterior relations – powerful hidden forces are at work, forces which rise to the surface of our lives in ways which disturb our peace of mind. This is true however slowly the changes take place. Sometimes the disturbance is obvious. It has been shown that this is a characteristic human reaction to situations of conflict. What is not so certain, however, is how long it lasts. It involves a definite mental operation aimed at the suppression of ordinary understanding, and the generation of new – false – cognitive evidence to replace it, which must be sustained for long periods. The evidence is that cognitive dissonance is more effective as a short-term aid to coping with stress than as a permanent strategy for survival. Perhaps this is because the business of kidding yourself about how you really feel is very tiring indeed. Perls, Hefferline and Goodman, the gestalt psychotherapists, attribute a good many of our psychological difficulties to the sheer exhaustion of our understanding because it has had to cope with denying its own perception of reality. It is as if we were flying on one engine instead of two – only rather than simply closing down on us, the 'dead' engine is trying as hard as possible to fly us backwards. With some people this kind of 'cognitive overload' results in depression, some become over-anxious, while others express their mental strain in bodily symptoms.

James, for example, developed a stammer about a year after he retired from his job with a car-sales company. He had worked for the same firm for almost forty years, the first twenty of which were on the 'floor', actually selling cars to customers. When he became an assistant manager, and even later, when he was manager and finally managing director, he enjoyed acting in his old role as salesman

17

whenever he had the chance: 'Got to keep my hand in, you know.' James's wife and children, knowing how much his job meant to him, were anxious at the thought of his approaching retirement: how would he cope without his beloved cars? 'No one can sell a car better than Dad,' his youngest daughter said, 'but everything comes to an end, I suppose.' James himself did not seem particularly bothered. He had bought a cottage in the country, one of his favourite spots, where he and his wife spent most weekends: 'Just getting into practice,' he said, 'there's a lot to be done in this garden. I'm looking forward to having the time to get properly down to it.'

In fact, when the time came, he didn't do very much in the garden. It was his wife who did most. James spent most of his time wandering round the cottage or 'just popping down to the village, dear'. What he actually did in the village she wasn't quite sure. It was a very small village: just the pub, the church and the post office-store. He never drank much at the pub, you couldn't buy much at the shop – perhaps he went into the church? One morning she followed him down. Sure enough, it was the church he went into. He was sitting at the front. She went down and sat by him. He wasn't expecting her, so he had no time to dry his tears. He was a man who never cried, so she asked him what was the matter. He smiled at her and said, 'I'm just thinking how lucky I am to be here at last.' It was not long after this that his stammer started. The vicar was looking for volunteers to read the lessons on Sunday. James would have liked to have had a go; after all, he was used to selling things. He was very distressed when he found he could no longer open his mouth without stammering. This alarmed him so much that he went to the village GP, and was referred back to the vicar, who found the time to listen to his story about the things that had been going on during the last few months. Here at last was somebody to whom James could speak honestly without having to pretend. The fact was that he had had no idea what it would be like, once he was retired. It was worse than he had imagined. First of all, there was the isolation from the life he had always known – 'I feel I've been stuck here like an old horse no one uses, in the paddock.' Worse than this was the overpowering feeling of uselessness, of having gifts and abilities that were suddenly surplus to requirements. For someone like James who had always been proudly aware of his own considerable talents, life in the cottage was so dramatic a reversal of the aims and objectives he had taken for granted as the expression of his own personality that he simply dare not take it in. He certainly could not let his wife and daughters know how he felt. The only thing to do was to stop feeling it! He sold the cottage to himself as if it were one of the cars on his beloved forecourt, and by doing so he forfeited the chance of discovering what life in the country was really like. He would have been better off hating where he was than refusing to be there at all. Only in the quiet seclusion of the church did he dare to let the mask slip. Three mornings a week, whenever the church was empty, he sat and suffered there. He was grateful for the opportunity, he told the vicar. The vicar listened and understood, and in so doing became more real. In time James was able to share all this with his wife, and even his daughters when they came to visit, bringing the grandchildren. The daughters were not surprised, knowing their father, that he had had a hard time adjusting to the change. As to the stammer, it took some months to go away. James went to a speech therapist who told him that he would go on stammering so long as he saw himself as someone who could no longer speak spontaneously and articulately. He had to learn to see his 'verbal fluency' as an inalienable attribute of his personality, and not as a skill belonging to a previous self. He was James, and James could flog ice-boxes to Eskimos. Everyone tried hard to reinforce this, particularly the vicar and congregation, and soon things began to get better.

Signs of distress occurring as a result of undisclosed psychological pressure are not always as easy to recognize as this. It was not difficult to see the connection between the sudden onset of stammering and grief at the loss of

19

the opportunity to be fluent in ways which contribute to one's satisfaction with oneself. Symptoms which occur in circumstances like this – what psychiatrists call hysterical symptoms – tend to reproduce their own causes in a kind of bodily picture-language, so that a person unconsciously directs attention to the nature of their problem without actually having to talk about it. Other people in similar situations, trying to escape the impact of these kinds of feelings, will become ill in ways which do not so readily reveal their origin: they may become depressed, or unnaturally impulsive and excitable, or over-anxious, or, with older people, confused and uncertain. The factor that ties all these reactions together is simply that they are all *reactions*: they all occur after retirement and are to be understood in connection with it, and with a general refusal on the part of the retired person to admit the connection. They are symptoms of intense psychological strain caused by turning a blind eye to whatever it is that is so very terrifying – in this case the prospect of retirement.

People tend to deceive themselves about retirement. Even if few of them go as far as James, they deceive themselves as to the extent of the psychological changes involved. They pretend that they can cope without any effort at all, whereas coping is always an effort, and often a considerable problem. When things go too far, and the person's state of mind and behaviour become a problem for themselves and to other people, the GP should be consulted, who may or may not refer them to a psychiatrist or clinical psychologist for treatment. This is considerably easier to advise than accomplish. People who are busy denying there is anything wrong with them do not welcome the idea of going to the doctor, but if you get them to talk about their pain you may release some of the pent-up emotion and render them more amenable. It may take a lot of effort, but it has to be done if they – and you – are to get the relief you both need. Most people, of course, do not need this kind of professional help. But the fact that some quite 'normal' people do highlights the perils implicit in life changes of this kind, and retirement in particular.

James could not stand the thought of losing his skill, so he didn't consider the matter at all. In the next chapters I shall be considering other things that get left out – power, status, role, continuity, hopefulness – with regard to all of which retirement involves or threatens a painful experience of loss. In every case the loss can prove pathological and needs professional help; in every case, however, the principal agent of healing is personal love. And a degree of justice.

This is very important. In theory, these things concern men and women equally. However, women still (at the moment) retire earlier than men, which may mean that some of them may have been retired for a number of years before their partners finally give up paid employment. Instead of working through the experience together, the woman finds herself having to adjust twice; her husband may have little awareness of, perhaps even sympathy with, a process he hasn't yet encountered, and may not want to have to face prematurely. When his turn comes to retire, however, she will be expected to use her experience to ease his passage. This is a real case of injustice. Another is the fact that work that goes on in the home is not considered to satisfy the 'work ethic' – is not real work, that is – in the same way as work outside the home. Unless women have two jobs, one inside and one outside, they are not regarded by a male-dominated society as doing any job at all! The result of this may be that women end up considerably more tired at retirement than men, despite currently being able to retire earlier. This will affect almost everything I intend to talk about in this book: women probably suffer more from lack of power, loss of status, role deprivation, and the like, than men do.

Certainly, the situation regarding women and retirement is pastorally very important indeed. The majority of the average congregation tend to be women in the second half of life, a category which includes church workers as well. Some of these people may be dreading the approaching retirement of their husbands, with the loss of daytime freedom that this will involve; on the other hand, they may have been looking forward to a deeper relationship once their husband has retired, only to find that his hobbies (and his dread of domesticity) render him even more unreachable than before. These are the kinds of retirement problem that come the way of the clergy rather than others, because the clergy have a great deal of contact with women who are passing through this stage in their lives. At the same time, the fact remains that they are particular versions of general problems which are characteristic of the entire human species when it is faced with having to adjust to this kind of change. At one level we are brought face to face with the difference between women and men as regards social organization and cultural expectation; at another level, a more basic one, we have to consider not difference but similarity.

2. Strength and Weakness

We all have a touch of Peter Pan in us. Nobody wants to grow old. Some people struggle against it more than others. It can be a destructive compulsion, because our own attitudes to life affect other people. 'It's just a matter of entertaining people, taking them out of themselves for a bit. I don't think there's anything else to it. All this metaphysical stuff's beyond me.' For many years Derek has combined his job as a social administrator with working as a creative therapist in a number of hospitals and clinics in the neighbourhood. In fact, Derek has played many roles in his life – as a factory worker, a novice monk, a bingo caller, a weekend soldier. He can wrap an audience, or a meeting, around his little finger with ease and style, so that they catch some of his virtuosity and find themselves responding in ways they wouldn't have believed possible. Derek draws great satisfaction from his ability to do this. This skill is central to his self-image.

Unfortunately, his private life has not been so successful. The power to carry an audience is not the same as the ability to sustain a marriage. He has been married three times. Since his last marriage failed he has had a succession of girlfriends. Those who know Derek are conscious of a certain credibility gap between his own account of these relationships, in which he is invariably loved and respected, the provider of stability and permanence which is rejected or unappreciated, and the man that they actually know, who always seems to be in the middle of an anguished struggle for emotional survival; and as he gets older, his need to find a lasting relationship grows more

23

desperate, and his unwillingness to admit his failure to do this even more marked. It is as if he is the victim of his own skill in appearances, his ability to influence people at a superficial level, bewitching them with the power of his personality like a brilliant child, shocking them on purpose for the sheer joy of getting away with it. Because he doesn't really involve himself, he can be as unkind as he wants, like a cruel child.

This, of course, is how Derek sees himself, as a person who manages to 'get by' by calling upon a precocious ability to avoid being tied down to anything or anyone, a skill he has always had, ever since he was a child. Rejection of 'all this metaphysical stuff' reflects an unwillingness to look deeper into the meaning of life and death. Particularly death. Derek can't allow himself to grow old, because his entire personality seems to him to depend upon staying his sprightly, indefatigable self. This year he is due to retire. He won't thank you for reminding him of the fact.

Derek's is an extreme case. His friends don't know how to help him, because he will never let them get close enough to do or say anything which might somehow reassure him, so that he might feel more able to face his fearfulness about growing old. If he was able to experience his terrors in symbolic, metaphoric form, if, in other words, he could himself benefit from the drama therapy he practices, perhaps he could begin to live a little nearer himself. The fact is that our inability to grow old involves other people very closely, because it is basically about the ability to draw strength from others through relationships – which, in turn, depends on being able to return it.

At the same time, it must be said that we live in an age which is particularly frightened of death, the idea itself, and all mention of the fact. So much of our effort to subdue the environment by industrialization, mechanization, automation, computerization, is motivated by the desire to perpetuate the world as we know it, defeating the forces of entropy, the tendency of all things to return to their original state of non-being. At its most creative and positive, the attempt to improve the human condition by mechanistic means has the same effect as merely protective or defensive stratagems do, for each simplification of human effort inches us further along the paths to Eden, a place which is no place at all for human beings to live in, rendering effort useless. People need to feel that the things they are involved in are useful and effective, so that in some way and to some degree the world is changed because of them. While we are doing something useful we feel we are staving off death, because we are aligned with the force that in the green fuse drives the flower – we are associated with and involved in the processes of life itself. The art of magic consists of having power over people and things without being in an honest relationship to them, so that people are inveigled and things manipulated, in contradiction to nature and human will. Because it is not a true expression of natural harmony, magic does not count as genuine work; which may be why Derek's desperate attempts at making contact with reality at the expense of human freedom never succeeded in keeping at bay his chronic fear of dying. There is no substitute for the real presence of living people when it comes to coping with our fears about death.

There has been much more discussion about death within the Christian Church during the last twenty years than there was in the first three-quarters of the century. When something is freely discussed, it loses the taboo quality that it would otherwise have and becomes that much less terrifying. Where fear of death is reduced, fear of growing old becomes a more accessible phenomenon, as more people are willing to admit to being affected by it to some extent. However strongly and firmly we believe in the Resurrection, fear of death is part of our heritage as human beings. The psychologist Otto Rank, who built on Freud's discoveries about the unconscious mind, maintained that our consciousness of vulnerability and our fear of death were the same thing, and that both stemmed from a terror of *life* which we learned at birth, when we were forcibly ejected from the happy security of the womb and exposed to the most traumatic change of all. Later writers, Janov and Lake among them, have traced psychological difficulties in children and adults to experiences sustained in the womb itself, physical and emotional wounds inflicted on the mother during pregnancy. Being born, however, is the most terrifying event of all, one, in fact, that we never forget. It is this, of course, that gives meaning to resurrection as an event in which we are involved, rather than an idea which we may or may not entertain. Because we participate psychologically in death *all our lives*, we know what it is that Christ conquered when he rose again on the third day. We may not have the faith to embrace this hope and let it transform our lives, but at least we are part of the ground in which the Cross is planted. Now that we can contemplate the origin of our fear of dying, that it is grounded in a fear of living, we can bring our weakness and fear to God as people who know what it is that they are doing. During the last twenty years, Christian theology has become more hard-hitting and more personal because of the rediscovery of the reality of our fear.

All the same, although some of us may be less afraid of death than people were thirty years ago, and many are less worried about talking about it, the fear of growing old remains. Socially speaking, old age has less prestige than it ever had. In a fiercely competitive society, in which commercial gain is the universal motive and success means pre-eminence in business or in one or another business-oriented activity, people who are old, too old to work, sometimes appear an irrelevance, sometimes, when they fall ill, an expensive irrelevance. Nobody wants this to happen to them.

So it is not simply fear of natural dying that colours our attitude to retirement. It is also fear of *social* death. Several of the men and women who were interviewed by David Karp in his investigation of attitudes held towards retirement by professional men and women (doctors, lawyers, university teachers) expressed a strong revulsion against having to stop working in ten or fifteen years' time. This reaction was strongest among those who were successful in their profession and in good health. Some people did in fact use the phrase 'social death' in this connection. These men and women saw their approaching retirement as simply too awful to contemplate. When you are as useful as these people felt themselves to be, and your sense of being important is corroborated by the people you move among and the places you visit, any diminishment of your social role presents itself as a definite threat. If life *is* this, then the remainder can only be death.

This is a very frightening state of mind to be in. The people concerned are not a typical cross-section of any community, even the American one from which they were drawn. All the same, the feelings expressed are widespread in Western society, and form the background against which any proclamation of the Gospel of Christ's Resurrection must take place. It is from social dying of the kind described here that Christ's followers rise again; and this social death is just as real, just as much a social fact, as the emotional death we have been considering. Possessions, prestige, power, the construction of a private social universe in which responsibility is kept at arms' length and one is protected from every imaginable source of discomfort and hardship as well as any kind of challenge – all serve as a way of armouring the self against the painful necessity to think about death. Illness, poverty, weakness, boredom, are all potent *memento mori*, whose effect must somehow be guarded against if peace of mind is to be preserved. Signs of increasing age are worst of all, growing more and more obtrusive, more and more limiting, until they can no longer be ignored. But of course the truth is that they can never really be ignored. Not successfully, that is. The peace of mind we seek in such a way always evades us. These things cannot be simply blotted out, they are part of our human condition and denial of them is denial of our very identity as people. Whatever we do, we do in their company: both they and the thought of them are evidence of the way we are.

In order that our feelings about these things may

27

change, we must be changed. We are free of them to the extent that we are transformed to a way of being in which our anxieties about being human no longer dominate our reaction to life and death. This revolution in our awareness does not make us less conscious of mortality. Indeed, by showing up our feeble denials for what they are, it brings home to us precisely what we were trying so hard to hide. We know that we are biological organisms, prone to all kinds of illness and disease, liable to misfortunes which can cripple our habitual way of coping with life and leave us penniless, naked and alone, delicately balanced psychic systems able to withstand only a limited degree of psychological strain, easily capable of becoming demented and finishing our lives no more capable of really personal relationship than we were when we started out.

Indeed, we know more than this. In disabusing ourselves about our ways of denying our real identity and hiding from the truth of our fearfulness, we open ourselves to a fuller understanding about the nature of sin. We know that we are sinful people pretending to be good, as well as weak people pretending to be strong. I don't think that this is because we became aware of God when we abandoned our defences against pain and anxiety. I'm sure that it is the other way round: the Holy Spirit enlightens us to God's presence and our need for him; our great need for his forgiveness is revealed to us in terms of all our spiritual needs and shortcomings. Spiritual here includes everything that is personal to us; it is a global forgiveness both of intentionally sinful acts and fears, doubts and anxieties which are themselves unintentional, but which nevertheless witness to the truth we are so eager to suppress, making clear the pathetic pride which poses as self-sufficiency – an ability to cope apart from God, which, if we are honest about ourselves, we simply do not really have. This is the real sin and it lies behind our attempts to distract our own attention, continually prevaricating rather than face what eventually must be faced: that we are simply no good without God, but he will only help us if we come clean. The point has been made many times, but never so well as by Paul Tournier. The businessmen, lawyers, surgeons and clergymen who put off retirement in a last frantic attempt 'to get their house in order' so that they can retire peacefully and in a blaze of glory like that of the setting sun would do well to think again. The anxieties which keep us pressing onwards, far from being a temporary fault in the system, are the truth about the situation, to be faced rather than avoided. If retirement is an uncomfortable reminder of the cost of being human and obeying the rules of one's own nature; if it reminds us of the approach of old age, with all its associations of illness, incapacity, loneliness and eventual death, then let us ask God for the courage to say, 'So be it.' Better to face this thing sooner than later. Derek devotes so much effort to keeping one step ahead of the one person who can tell him who he really is and why he really need not run at all.

He is not alone in this. In one form or another, fear of death is probably the most widespread reason for not wanting to retire, although you would go a long way before finding anybody who admitted it about themselves. In many cases the fear itself, and the feelings about retirement thrown up by it, are completely denied, in the sense of being repressed and consequently consigned to unconsciousness. Sometimes thoughts about the implications of making this very definite step, passing this obvious milestone on the road towards old age 'and what lies beyond' have arisen and even been expressed. People and circumstances differ considerably, as we shall see. There are many other reasons for our unwillingness to lay down the reins, some of which we shall be looking at in the following chapters. Indirectly they all relate to what we have been talking about here. The same rule applies to them as applies here. It is this: in the context of God's transforming and renewing love, revealed in the dying and rising again of Jesus, our fears are without basis in fact. It is because we do not always completely trust God that we tend to be frightened of the *implications* of changes affecting our present condition. The *experience* of drastic change itself, however, is always painful and disturbing, liable to put even the strongest and simplest faith to the test. At the same time, even this experience is destined in the long run to strengthen faith.

Rank called the state of mind that refuses to admit its own vulnerability 'causa sui': 'he is responsible for himself', 'he made himself'. Causa sui means that it is up to us to keep living because we have somehow thought ourselves into being, and any admission of frailty is a surrender of our integrity as human beings. If we go on like this we stand in danger of losing our immortality. Rank points out that this attitude has been responsible for some major acts of courage, as well as for countless minor deceits, attempts to deceive ourselves and manipulate others. It is not, and never can be, however, the Christian way of dealing with life's problems and facing its challenges. For one thing, it never works. Real power over death comes when we understand this.

However much we acknowledge our dependence on God, we are still free to exercise authority on our own account. This delegated authority belongs to us, as Christ belongs to us and we to him. To enjoy it properly, we must use it properly.

We don't always have the chance, however. Penny retired early from a job in which she had carried a good deal of personal responsibility. 'In the early days, I was very anxious about finance and how to spend my time. I suggested to the clergy I might do more in the church, but I wasn't given anything. I have a close friend who is a nun, and she is my spiritual adviser, and she said I must be very relaxed and patient, and wait to see what God sent my way while enjoying my "freedom". But I couldn't really settle down. For instance, I had two blouses cut out, but I didn't sew them. It is only this month when there is less church activity that I have begun to work on them.'

Penny's church is extremely active, yet it appears that there was no way in which someone who had recently had to give up responsibility in the business world could help to run it. Even though their health may be excellent, newly retired people are weak and dependent, because their hard-earned skills are made to look irrelevant. The nun's advice was sound but, like so much Christian counselling, it turned out to be impossible to carry out: enjoying freedom is an active state, relaxing is a passive one. You can learn to relax, and it will certainly help you to feel more peaceful, but it won't take away any real factual anxieties you may have about how worthwhile your life is, or how capable you are of doing the things that 'normal' employed people do. It won't make you feel strong and in control again. Only being given a job will do that.

Penny doesn't say how many clergy there were, how many of them she asked, or how often. Unfortunately one has to make the point, which may seem strange, because in some churches, the more clergy there are the harder it is to get through to the one you want, the one you should have asked in the first place. Because she says 'the clergy' I'm tempted to think this is a large church and unfortunately, large, well-organized churches tend to be exceptionally well insulated from their members.

Perhaps this church is not a bit like this. Perhaps I'm being totally unfair. But even if it's not, others are. Penny is particularly unfortunate, because she doesn't belong in a particular social grouping. She is neither a business person nor a (conventionally) retired one. It's a striking fact that churches which have most to offer to individuals (and to the individual in all of us) tend to cater for groups – families, children, 'young people', wives. As yet, there is no group for those who have taken early retirement on health or other grounds, yet they need help more than any other section of the retired population. In an article in *Group*, the Journal of Group Psychotherapy, Dr John Salvendy describes how 'whatever terms their retirement recommendations were couched in, [such people] felt diminished' because they 'lacked the face-saving protection that mandatory retirement offers to others'. Many of these who retire early miss the stimulation of being with others, and many feel guilty at having 'quit the game before the final whistle'. They feel that 'if they had "really" tried, they could have succeeded longer in their jobs'. All this may be quite unrealistic. To the people concerned, however, it is a psychological fact. This group, above all, need to be helped to see themselves as contributing usefully to the church community. They illustrate the fact that the *circumstances* of a person's retirement have a direct bearing on the way he or she sees the world, and consequently interprets what happens in church.

One thing Penny could do would be to ask the clergy if she might set up a group for retired people within the parish. If she were able to do this it might help her a good deal, because it would draw on something she has come to know quite a lot about. Certainly, it would be yet another group. This time, however, it would be for a very specific purpose, that of providing support and a new kind of identity for people who really would benefit from a chance to meet together on a systematic basis. It seems that the most effective kind of therapy for people who are finding retirement hard to cope with takes place in groups, which meet to play games, make up stories and talk about the past. Reminiscing is a great source of encouragement, when it is allowed and enjoyed. Some theatre companies exist specifically for this purpose, acting out the audience's memories for them on the stage, though there is no need to be as ambitious as this; story-telling mime, drawing, role-play, are all ways of sharing the past and establishing its reality.

It has been remarked that such groups, although set up to build confidence and security by remembering the past, often find themselves discussing the subject of death. Confidence, founded in the past, can be built on for the future. The notion of a story requires the idea of an ending; my journey through life implies my destination. I would rather think about it now, in context and in company, than remember it when I am alone. In this way, the corporate denial of death is undermined, and the power of the Church's teaching about the Resurrection reasserted. Loneliness, sharing, spiritual comfort, and faith: these are things involved in the formation of such groups. They should, of course, be seen in the context of the total management a person may require upon retirement, including issues of physical health, adequate diet and suitable housing, and opportunities for exercise and recreation, matters not directly within the church's remit, as far as direct provision is concerned, but involving at least a watching brief from the congregation and clergy. In some parts of the country professionally run groups exist under the general description of 'Brief Group Psychotherapy for the Retired'. Details of these can usually be obtained from your GP.

With regard to learning to relax, it seems that the more we are allowed to take part in activities that give us emotional and intellectual satisfaction – in other words, that we ourselves would choose to take part in – the less anxiety we experience, and this would certainly seem to be the case with retired people. A study carried out by Jane Kaufman demonstrated that 'the greater the leisure participation in a retired population . . . the lower the anxiety level'. (Kaufman concentrated on the relaxing effect of having taken part in sport, but the crucial factor was the level of involvement in a particular pursuit, so perhaps going to church-related activities would satisfy her criteria.) To relax is to go on enjoying whatever to you seems to be worthwhile!

What Penny is searching for is the positive affirmation of her place in, and consequently importance to, society. She is not alone in this, of course. There are many millions like her throughout the world. Her experience of early retirement, when she is still able to contribute so much to life, makes her case the more dramatic. We see her at her weakest. Unless the church persists in de-skilling her she can only grow stronger. As the average age of the population rises, and people tend to stay active longer, so that the need for people to stop working in their fifties and sixties for health reasons decreases, it becomes more and more important to think in terms of retirement *to* rather than retirement *from*. Retirement has always been a

33

staging-post in life. More attention now needs to be paid to the retired person's new life as a contributing member of society. Post-retirement provision should be seen in terms of allowing and encouraging people to develop as people, not merely keeping them occupied. 'The retirement event itself can be construed as the document of transfer,' says Neil McClusky: 'the transfer is a transition into a new phase of mature adult life with its own special expectancies, tasks and challenges.'

Not everyone is willing to receive help, however. Asking for help is frequently seen as a way of conferring power upon others – power over oneself.

3. Power and Authority

This chapter is about the sense of individual authority, the feeling that people have of being in charge so that they can throw their weight about if they should happen to want to. It is also about status, an idea that is central to any discussion of retirement.

Audrey retired at sixty. As a teacher she could have retired some years earlier, but she was deeply involved in her job, and strongly resisted the idea of giving it up. She used to say, whenever the subject came up, that she had no reason to want to give up work, having no family of her own, unlike her married friends – 'this is my family, here, I don't need another one'. Circumstances, plus her own determination to stay put, led to her spending all her working life in one school, so that she ended her teaching career as headteacher in the school she had arrived at as a student forty years earlier. A good few tears were shed at her retirement, by pupils as well as teachers. It was, after all, very much her school.

Actually, Audrey did have a family. When not at school her job was to look after her aged mother. Although still not confined to her bed, her mother was very frail, both physically and mentally, and depended almost entirely on Audrey and Audrey's ability to organize an auxiliary support network for times when she was not there herself. Now, of course, she was always there; and so was her mother. Instead of five hundred people of whom she was in charge, she now had just one. She did not intend to do this job any less professionally than the other, however. In a way it was a much easier job, because, whereas there was always a degree of opposition at school, either from rebellious children or insubordinate ('disloyal') staff, her mother could put up no resistance at all. Neighbours soon began to pass remarks about how thoroughly organized Audrey's mother had become. She always looked neat, her hair brushed and her clothes freshly laundered. They had many opportunities to observe such things, as Audrey rarely left her mother alone at home, always taking her with her when she went shopping or paid social calls: 'This is Mother. Look how well I care for her.' The old lady did not seem very grateful, however. Whereas she always used to be cheerful and sociable, she rarely looked happy nowadays. In fact, she was finding this degree of attention on Audrey's part difficult to cope with. She never had time by herself, to potter round the house and do all the little things she used to do when her daughter was out of the way. She never had time to be herself any more. She felt that life had begun to consist of mindless conformity to her daughter's ideas and intentions. She felt herself being made into a 'lovely old lady, such a credit to her daughter, who looks after her'. She hadn't much mind left – at least, she felt she hadn't – but what there was, was hers. Why was Audrey such a bully? Why couldn't she leave her alone?

Audrey would have been very surprised, and very hurt, if she had known that her mother was feeling like this. She noticed that the old lady seemed quieter than she had been, but she put it down to old age. After all, what had the poor dear to live for? The least she could do was to look after her properly, really care for her, so that her last years could be lived with dignity. Once, when she was still teaching, she had come home to find her mother wandering round the garden, still in her nightie. She said she was 'picking flowers'; her face and hands were covered in soil and her white hair was blowing all over her face. Audrey was both shocked and terrified. At least now she could make sure that this sort of thing would never happen again. At this point, she began to be aware of her mother's rising tide of resentment. However, it did not deter her. So long as she was in charge, she would see to it that her mother did as she was told.

Audrey's story is an example of what is often the case when authority degenerates into power. The difference between power and authority is a very important one. It can be expressed as follows:

> *Power* is 'the ability of its holder to exact compliance or obedience of other individuals to his will on whatsoever basis'.
>
> *Authority* is 'an attribute of social organization in which command inheres in the recognition of some greater competence lodged either in the person or in the office itself'.
>
> (*The Fontana Dictionary of Modern Thought*)

Many writers, notably Otto Rank in the nineteenth century and Peter Berger in the twentieth, have described how people protect themselves from one another by creating institutions and then proceeding to give them legal authority which is binding upon everybody. Rank is quite explicit about the reason for doing this: it is because the heads of families wished to preserve their own domestic omnipotence and were willing to yield any extra power they had to support a system which would allow them to do exactly as they liked at home. 'Authority has a kind of holiness that power does not possess. This is due to the way it originates.' For common security, power among families (not among family *members*) is shared by being projected on to governments, legal systems, churches, hospitals, universities and schools, and so on, which become endued with a kind of ultimate value, so that to disobey their rulings would be disastrous, not merely at the level of practical arrangements for living or the preservation of private property and public peace, but also at the level of the meaning and purpose of being alive at all. Sometimes psychologists and sociologists seem to believe that God is a kind of divine policeman, created by men and women in order to preserve public order. Sometimes Christian people appear to support this view. However, with regard to the state, as distinct from God, but vested by human beings with some of his authority,

37

there seems to be a lot of sense in Rank's judgement that 'our idea of it is due in the last analysis to [mankind's] fear of this naked power, which we need to cloak in various kinds of justification, *and which represents the actual life-force itself*'.

Wanting power is fundamental to being human. The will to be important, to have authority, to exercise power in some guise or another, either direct or reflected, is part of the need for self-expression, the energy which in the green, human plant 'drives the fuse'. Freud referred to it as the 'libido', a pleasure-principle, using it to explain, directly or indirectly, every human phenomenon. This is why, once the constraints of authority have been lifted, the phenomenon of power always presents itself in some form or another. Once it was no longer under the control of school discipline, power became 'a family matter'.

In a sense, of course, it had always been this. When she came to even the score with her mother, Audrey, like every daughter and son, had a good deal of ground to cover. 'So long as the parents are in power, so long is the child's assertion of itself incomplete' (Anthony Storr). This is not to say that there was any conscious intention on her part to repay old debts, although the memory of ancient wrongs may from time to time have emerged, as it does with most of us. Nor was Audrey conscious of wielding power over her mother. Certainly not! What she felt and was expressing was *concern*. She would not have liked to think that she had power over anybody at all. Authority, yes, power no. This is understandable, of course, authority being the acceptable face of power. Power is selfish and unruly, whereas authority is always respectable and sometimes generous. Authority had guided her actions while she was a schoolteacher. Now, however, she was mainly a daughter again, back in the world of power, but this time possessing what as a child she had only dreamed about. In fact, Audrey had more need of finding scope for her feeling of 'power-potential' than she had the actual desire to dominate others. Her upbringing had provided her with both security and freedom; she had much to thank her mother for. She was quite willing and able to share power; and when she found a retirement job that gave scope to her talent for organization a good deal of the pressure on her mother was lifted.

It is only among those who are emotionally deprived that the pure, unadulterated urge for power flourishes. This is true of both individuals and groups. Abraham Maslow relates the desire for dominance to feelings of self-confidence and self-esteem; it is individuals who are less secure who seek to reassure themselves by exercising power over others. In *The Informed Heart*, Bruno Betelheim describes how easily, among one particular group of people, total powerlessness led directly to the abuse of power:

> All ruling prisoners [in the Nazi concentration camps] were responsible for the destruction of some prisoners, to save themselves, their friends, or other members of their group. The ambiguous attitude of the prisoner élite towards other prisoners went beyond motives of safety, or economic and social advantages. Often equally attractive was the psychological appeal of power.

It seems that human beings can be so stripped of dignity and the opportunity to be human, so preoccupied with the sheer mechanics of staying alive, that their sole means of self-expression is confined to keeping one step ahead at whatever cost. Once having gained this kind of primitive, feral dominance, only death can dislodge us. The life stories of freedom-fighters who eventually become dictators serve to illustrate the point, ending as they do with their bodies being dragged feet-forward from the rubble.

The purpose of all this has been to show how important the possession of power is to us, and how we cling to it. We are more likely to think in terms of status than power. Status refers directly to power exercised within an organized social environment of a particular kind. It is a dimension of social stratification in that it refers to a view of society in which degrees of social 'weight' have been carefully distinguished. In other words, it is a way of marking someone's place on a scale of comparative social values. One's dress, conversation, accent, table manners, are signs of one's status within a particular hierarchy of social roles. Outside the scope of that hierarchy the message loses meaning, like being in an expensive French restaurant never before having crossed the Channel. Status signifies one's place in a social order; there may be many such orders running concurrently, so that person occupies a different position, and enjoys a different degree of comparative privilege, according to each – for instance, the truck driver who is a PhD.

In pre-modern societies status was usually accorded with regard to birth. Nowadays, however, social prestige differs according to a person's position on a ranked scale of occupations. Although not so highly ranked as it was, and certainly less regarded than it should be, teaching still enjoys a good deal of social respect. As headteacher of a school, Audrey not only felt that she was in a position of some authority, she also knew herself to be a person of some social status. The two things are similar, but not the same. By the exercise of proper authority her personal being was established at a certain social level. On the map which showed where things happened, she could be located quite easily. She was an important part of the world's work.

No wonder she did not find retirement easy. She had been 'reduced to the ranks', which in our society tend to be lower for women than for men! She had been a headteacher for many years. In fact, it was in this form, as lack of status, that she experienced powerlessness most vividly. All retirements are different, but in some important ways all are similar. All involve a loss of instrumentality, a diminished sense of participation in the way things are organized. Even small cogs in large machines may have this sense of powerlessness when they are replaced. Even small cogs (to stretch the metaphor) make the most effective use of any instrumental effect they may still produce; in this case the domination and manipulation of the woman with whom she lived. People tend to behave selfishly when their behaviour seems to be rapidly decreasing in its power to change the situation in which they find themselves, in any significant way.

At this point Audrey's situation began to show signs of improving, and this made a considerable difference to her attitude towards her mother. At first the old lady wondered what had happened to her daughter to make her so much easier to live with. They began to enjoy doing things together: working in the garden, pottering around the house. They even visited the neighbours without her feeling awkward, as she used to do, when it seemed that her daughter was presenting her for inspection. It was hard to put her finger on it; things just seemed easier all round. Not so much pressure. She had always loved Audrey of course. That went without saying. Now she found herself liking her as well. It was all rather remarkable, and rather wonderful. She didn't say anything to Audrey, not in so many words. Nor did she try to analyse what was happening – better just to enjoy the difference. She had the idea, though, that it had something to do with church. They always went to church together, and always had done, since they used to go as a family, when her husband was alive. She always enjoyed the service. Audrey, on the other hand, seemed to go out of habit rather than because she really wanted to.

What had happened – this was what she said – was that the message about what was involved in being a Christian had got through to Audrey. It had got through when she needed most to hear it. 'My strength is made perfect in weakness.' The power of Christians is the Holy Spirit, the Spirit of the one who, though the divine nature was always his, 'did not think to snatch at equality with God, but made himself nothing, assuming the nature of a slave'. Audrey had heard these words many times, and had always loved them. Sometimes they had made her cry, if she was feeling 'down'. They usually made her feel humble. Now, for the first time, they made her feel strong. *Made himself* humble'; '*assumed the nature* of a slave'. This, then, was what people meant when they talked about the 'power' of the gospel: not simply being swept away by your feelings, but discovering the strength of Christ which could never be defeated because it had already given itself away, and given itself away *to you*.

That morning Audrey regained her authority. She did this by her willingness to share in the authority of Christ. This meant that other ways of expressing her will, other sources of power, were to be consciously repudiated, even as in Christ they had been finally defeated. The New Testament is in no doubt at all that these other ways of overcoming one's feelings of inferiority and powerlessness are not of God. In fact, they are Satanic, although the ways that they find expression are all too human. Satan is not any kind of person at all, not even a monstrously bad one. When we talk about him, we are describing an anti-personal force, the aim of which is to use human personhood to its own ends, which are always anti-personal, because they are anti-God. The best way of opposing the Person is by using his creation against him – in this way Satan talks about God's closest concern, using the language of his own Being to do so.

Or would be, if Christ had not defeated him. Since Christ's victory on the Cross, men and women have possessed the truth. Specifically, they possess it in their own personhood; in other words, in their being together as persons. The Christian Church, the fellowship and body of Christ, is the prototype of the ideal society. As such it has an inalienable authority, the authority of its founder. This is why Harvey Cox says that its task is to be a 'cultural exorcist', with each congregation engaged in the task of realizing the defeat of Satan. This is certainly St Paul's view: 'our fight is not against human foes, but against cosmic powers, against the authorities and potentates of this dark world, against the superhuman forces of evil in the heavens'. At the cosmic level Satan is outfaced by Christ, who fills his void with life; at the level of individual men and women the urge for dominance is redeemed and relationship, the authority of love, transforms our social life.

At least we hope it does. We all know churches where power is misused, where the vicar blackmails the congregation, the elders bully the minister, and goodwill and the willingness to serve are ruthlessly exploited by the PCC. In my experience, they are not the majority; and even where such things do happen, their nature is revealed and their origin repudiated as they come beneath the authority of word and sacrament. Again, there are some churches where the message about our participation in Christ, and therefore in God, is played down to suit our ideas of what is likely. Perhaps this is to spare us the embarrassment of failing to grasp such a mind-shattering idea. Mind-shattering and genius-confounding: something we could never have thought out, never mind carried out, by ourselves. These reasonable churches seem to give the impression that God has somehow to be persuaded to give us the authority we need in order to do his work in the world. We do not earn that authority any more than we deserve it. We simply have it. But try telling some churches and church folk that! They are not the kind of church that a disempowered person needs. Such a person ought to be surrounded by no less than the authority of the risen Christ so that he or she may be helped to reinterpret weakness in terms of strength, loss of status in terms of eligibility for the kingdom of heaven. If such a thing had happened to Audrey earlier in her story both she and her mother might have been spared a breakdown in their relationship which came near to being a permanent estrangement. As it was, the human spirit, deprived of creative expression in the form of legitimate authority, became for the time being the exercise of pure power. I am not suggesting that this was evil or Satanic in itself, only that it was open to corruption by evil. The relationships that join us together in our personal lives are open to the influence of a cosmic principle that constantly fights against relationship. There is a tendency for us to use authority but to *be used by* power. Satan turns us inwards to what appears to us to be to our own advantage, using self-interest to destroy what love and generosity strive to

43

build up. Satan's *modus operandi* is clearly revealed in the ideas he presented to Jesus in the wildnerness, three fundamental forms of selfishness or areas of exploitation of power, concerning our relationship with nature, our fellow men and women, and God. This is pretty inclusive; and we may depend on it that whatever provides an opportunity will be snapped up, however trivial the occasion may seem. With three exceptions, Satan is no respecter of persons. It seems that there is a good deal of truth in the old saying about him 'finding work for idle hands'!

4. The Cost of Change

This chapter is about loss and grief. You are recommended to read more about this. There are many books available on the subject, notably those by John Bowlby, Colin Murray Parkes, and Peter Speck, apart from ones which are specifically about bereavement, or the care of terminally ill people. These books are worth reading in any case because, generally speaking, when it comes to learning about life, the things we worry about most are the ones we spend least time and effort studying. These are books about life, the part that frightens us. We cannot afford to ignore them.

Now is a good time to read about this. Even if we are looking forward to retiring, or have just retired and are settling down happily into a new way of life, the idea of potentially difficult, even painful, change is one that is close to our minds. No doubt we shall need some persuasion to bring it even closer. Pain is precisely what we want to avoid; change (because it tends to involve a degree of pain) is what we hope to keep to a minimum. We're doing very well, thank you very much. We don't need to go looking for trouble. Death as yet is not the issue for us. For the time being we would prefer to leave it alone. We may feel this very strongly indeed, particularly if we are finding the changes in our life more painful than we expected them to be. How can this be a good time to read about the very thing we want to forget? We need books to take our minds off things, books to help us forget, not ones that simply pile on the agony.

In fact, books about grief and loss have a different effect.

First of all, they perform a psychotherapeutic task precisely because they help us to think consciously about a whole area of life that always causes us a degree of unconscious pain; something that is awkward and frightening to think about but much more painful, giving rise to much more anxiety, when we don't think about it, but run away from it as if it were the very worst thing that could happen. We need books about death to enable us to face the reality of what happens to us in life.

Many writers on the subject, notably Bowlby and Speck, have drawn attention to the way in which things that happen to us in the course of our lives are affected by the way in which we protect ourselves from any conscious suggestion that we shall one day actually die. Anything that disturbs the normal course of our life, any change in our circumstances which affects in a recognizable way the way in which we go about the business of living, any minor shock or major adjustment, tends to remind us of the greatest change, the biggest existential event of all. Our road through life is pitted with a succession of minor dyings.

And, of course, minor resurrections. According to John Roebuck, people see retirement as a transition to old age. It is equally a passage into new life. If to read a book about dying is a reminder of one's own death, to have read it is the mark of survival, one more example of the victory of meaning over chaos. To have had the courage and the common sense to take seriously the things that we would rather not face is not to have been spared the pain of actually experiencing their presence in our lives. When the even course of living is radically interrupted we are bound to suffer, whether or not we have succeeded in getting used to the idea of suffering, either in general or in this particular case. Indeed, we may know very well what we are in for, but this will not stop it hurting when it arrives. The only thing is, we shall now have some idea as to *why* it hurts so much, and this will certainly be an advantage, if we will let it be so. Whatever happens, we must not try to explain everything away to ourselves or to anyone else.

What we learn from books will help us think; it will not stop us feeling. We cannot bypass the processes which cause so much agony to others, using our psychological expertise to sidestep the painful effects that we have read about. Whether or not we succeed in bringing our ego-defensiveness into play, the fact of loss will always reach us and we shall suffer the results of traumatic change taking place in our lives. It is in retrospect, when we look back at what has been happening to us, that we remember what we read and are relieved by the knowledge that we were not alone in our suffering, even though we may have felt as though we were. Such books are commentaries rather than handbooks: in other words, they tell us what loss and grief are about. They cannot really tell us how to cope with them. This is their message: that there is no growth without change, and no change without pain. Sometimes the pain involved is the pain of dying.

This in itself is enough, however, to change the way we think about life. Fifty years ago death was a taboo subject, except when it was treated under the protective guise of fiction. Otherwise it was kept firmly within the private domain. The resurgence of interest in death which is current nowadays probably originated in work carried out by Colin Murray Parkes and John Bowlby in the early 1960s concerned with the psychology of mourning. About this time Robert Lambourne and Michael Wilson, working at Birmingham University, were beginning to think in a theological way about the experience of human grieving. Theological journals which for twenty-five years had not carried a single article about death or mourning suddenly started to devote whole issues to these neglected subjects.

The effect of all this has been to change other people's experience of our mourning. Because others are aware of what people go through when they suffer the effects of loss, they are more sympathetic towards us than they would have been. They do not exhort us to behave normally when we are overcome with emotion, or praise us

47

for being 'our old selves again', or tell people 'how well we're taking it', just when crying is the only thing that would give us any kind of release. Instead, they have learned to be with us while we take things at our own speed, encouraging us to talk about the one that all this distress is about; holding our hand amid the chaos, stroking our head amid the hopelessness, hearing the anger, giving it the courage to speak, working with us to shape a kind of survival, a place where past and future may at length be contemplated within the same idea, spoken about in the same sentence; working, that is, towards the healing of a story. All this is of inestimable worth. It is due to what is to be learned from books about grief and loss, and about the lesser deaths as well as the greater ones. Every experience of real personal change involves the same kind of dynamism as the one recognized by Murray Parkes and Bowlby, and by Elizabeth Kubler-Ross in the circumstances surrounding human death.

This time of chaos is crucial for real change to take place. As I have said elsewhere:

> For the new situation to 'live', the old one must 'die'. Thus there is always a crucial point 'between', a point representing the condition after the old state of affairs has come to an end and before the new one has actually begun. This is the moment of real change, the pivotal moment that has no movement of itself, but permits movement to take place.

The process of unlearning which leads to this is painfully slow even when the state of affairs to which it refers has changed quite suddenly, as is often the case in bereavement. In counselling bereaved people most of the time is taken up with this process of unlearning the past in opposition to the self-protective urge to cling to it, thus denying the fact of change.

Writers on bereavement have long been aware of the general 'shape' it tends to assume. For example, Robert Hobson says that 'a comparative cross-cultural study of death rites reveals a sequence of three stages, separation, transition and reincorporation which roughly correspond to the three phases of individual mourning'. Hobson refers to these as 'shock', 'disorganization' and 'reorganization'. There may be more phases within the total reaction to loss as this has been analysed by psychologists and sociologists, but it seems to be widely agreed that the overall process is divisible into a period of shocked withdrawal, the immediate reaction to a painful loss; a period of confusion and suspense of all purposeful activity; a period of renewal, reconstruction and gradual reinvestment in life. In other words, there is a movement towards a dead centre and then outwards again. Geoffrey Gorer, whose book *Death, Grief and Mourning in Contemporary Britain* was a seminal work for all modern writers, says that

> Judging by my interviews and the range of rituals and practices reported by historians and anthropologists, it would seem that most adult mourners pass through three stages: 1) a period of shock, usually between the occurrence of the death and the disposal of the body; 2) a period of intense mourning, accompanied by withdrawal of much attention from the external world and by such psychological changes as disturbed and restless sleep, failure of appetite and loss of weight; 3) a final period of re-established physical homeostasis [balanced interaction], sleep and weight again established, interest directed outwards.

The instinct of people who have suffered loss is to move directly on from stage one to stage three without passing through stage two. It seems to be characteristically human to think of things that happen to us in terms of twos, dividing triads into pairs of dyads. We like things to be definite, cancelling out 'grey areas'. But it is precisely these intermediate areas that allow our understanding to be definite – they actually separate events from each other and let them stand as themselves. In this case the intermediate second stage divides 'before' from 'after', establishing the reality of each and allowing us to find a way of coming to terms with them as part of a real state of affairs existing in the world. Stage two is, very simply, the time of unlearning. It is also, from the point of view

49

of the creative process, the time of learning (or at least the time that makes learning possible). But it is a very painful phase to be in, and we go out of our way to bypass it, asserting intellectual control over turbulent feelings which would be much better left to find their own resolution in their own time. The mind is very good at this kind of confidence trick: the skill of people involved in counselling the bereaved often consists of shepherding them towards the chaos they are so eager to deny, which separates them from recovery as if it were a river rushing down a chasm which cannot, but must, be crossed.

Every experience of real change involves the fording, rather than the bridging, of a river. In all places in the world, at every period of time, the human tendency to try to leap the gap from the old into the new without passing through what lies between and separates them has been taken into account in rites of passage, ritual complexes which reproduce in threefold symbolic form the circumstances of real change. The funeral rite is a vivid example of this, although all kinds of important 'changes of direction' in the lives of individuals were recognized and established socially by passage rites. In many cultures the central movement of the funeral consisted of the wake, the most vivid expression of personal and social chaos. (Irish wake customs traditionally portrayed the total inversion of all established values expressed in games of monumental perversity.) Throughout the world funeral rites demonstrated the real shape of grief, moving from 'dismissal' via 'chaos', to 'reintegration', bringing home the reality of the event upon which its true survival depends. This is the purpose of religious ritual throughout the world. The famous sociologist of religion, Max Weber, maintained that ritual asserted the reign of universal law over 'the changes and chances of this mortal life' by its ability to contain chaos within itself by presenting human reality within the context of the divine.

Rehabilitation and retirement are both situations which depend upon an experience of death and renewal, in which we die to the old state of affairs so that we can live to the new one. However dramatic it may appear, this is basic to their structure as experienced events. For some it will be an easier death than for others. It should be pointed out, however, that those who have an easy passage, while being spared a good deal of agony, may also lose the chance of new and exciting beginnings. Those who are finding life very difficult at present, who having once left their familiar ways can't find their feet at all and heartily wish they might return to the way of life that was second nature to them – these may receive some comfort from the fact that what they are going through is an essential part of the process of unlearning the past, which constitutes their initiation into the future.

To unlearn is not to forget, however, although it may feel as though forgetting were the principal danger, to be avoided at all costs. If we let go of the past, what shall we do? What shall we cling to? The future is not to be trusted, as our recent experience shows only too well. And as for the present . . . All this, however, is part of the immediate experience of loss, rather than of the underlying psychological process that we are involved in. In this, continuity is as important as change. As Kelly says, the psychology of grief and loss 'is concerned with finding better ways to help a person reconstrue his life so that he need not be the victim of the past'. The mind is always at work on its picture of life. When the picture is thrown out of focus, distorted or even partly destroyed, the same skills are ready to repaint it – in a new way, perhaps, with a new subject, but using the same pigments. The fact is that we only experience change within the context of continuity. The mind's bias towards inventing and perpetuating structures is the reason why this kind of change is experienced as what indeed it is, an overloading of the system which may or may not provoke a breakdown of its immediate ability to cope with its job of making sense of things. In any case, it is unlikely to have a permanent effect within a set-up which is basically designed to cope with change.

When we re-learn what has been unlearned, it is as if

51

we were retranslating the past into a language which can be used for the future, as a source of meaning in life. Real changes in the way we understand and experience life only happen when the new has somehow been accommodated within the framework of the old, built into the fabric of a personal story as a change in the action: a new direction, but the same plot. Only a strong story-line can sustain real changes in the plot. Most of us have put in a good deal of hard work since we were children wearing our personal narratives, which, as we shall see in the next chapter, constitute the foundation of our self-image. It is this tough fabric of interwoven ideas and experiences that bears the weight of changes that take place in our lives. If the change is an important one, particularly if it is unexpected, we may feel that our narrative strength is simply unequal to the task; we simply cannot cope with the necessity to take it in. Perhaps every really new event in our lives has this effect on us; if it doesn't, then it isn't really new or really an event. The plot shifts, but the story continues, even though, for us, the world has stopped. Here are some brief examples of interrupted stories:

Simon was eighty-five years old when he died. He and his wife, Janet, lived the last few years of their lives in an almshouse about fifteen miles away from the farm where Simon had worked for many years as a labourer. Simon had never intended to retire at all, so it was a surprise when his employer, the farmer, suggested that seventy years old was getting on a bit to be still working as hard as he was. At first he couldn't manage to cope with the idea at all: 'I just don't waste time thinking about it.' He and his wife wept a good deal when it came to moving house, though it wasn't like either of them to show emotion. They wondered what was happening to them. There wasn't anybody to talk to about things. At this point it occurred to the farmer that he might as well let Simon and Janet stay on in the farm cottage, so he went along to see them at the almshouse. Janet would have liked to go, but Simon refused: 'No point in moving twice.' He was obviously still angry with the farmer for 'sacking' him.

He took to making solitary walks through the village. On one of these he discovered a pub that took his fancy. There was a bloke there round about his age, who had been a gamekeeper on an estate near Simon's farm. People in the pub used to like to hear him talking about 'the old days'. He got Simon talking, and seemed interested, for he'd never worked on a farm himself.

It was some time before Janet got around to asking him where he went when he went out by himself. At first she was relieved to get him out of the house: 'It's better than having him brooding about here.' She guessed that he went to a pub, but she didn't know which one. She knew that things were getting better when he asked her to go with him. 'Come on, lass. They like me up there. I'm the only one that's worked on a farm, you see.'

Frederick was a lawyer. He retired two years ago, at the age of sixty. He and his sister, Alethea, live in a comfortable Edwardian house in a suburb of a Yorkshire town. Fred and Alethea love the town, which, says Fred, is 'about the right size for knowing people'. Certainly there was not very much competition from other law firms, and Fred was able to feel that he occupied a position of some social importance in the town. Alethea, too, was well known locally. She was a violinist and always had several would-be pupils on her waiting-list.

Fred had made considerable plans for his retirement. Violin teachers were always in demand, he said, so Alethea was as mobile as he would be. They had owned a small house in Cumberland for several years, and used to use it for holidays. Now it would really come into its own as their retirement home. Fred felt he was being entirely reasonable about this. He was looking forward to retiring; although he enjoyed his job, he felt he had been a lawyer for long enough: 'I shan't be sorry to retire.' Alethea wasn't so sure. She had a lot of contacts locally, and liked to keep up with her former pupils' progress. They decided

53

to compromise: Fred would go up to Cumberland by himself, Alethea following when she felt more like moving.

As it turned out, Fred only stayed for a couple of weeks. They were some of the worst weeks he ever spent anywhere. He couldn't settle to doing anything at all but simply wandered about the cottage garden. He couldn't stand being in the house alone. 'It's all right getting away, but not *that* far away,' he said. 'There's much too much of me invested down here. That place is all right for weekends.' He had always said that he didn't want to hang round the office being a nuisance once he retired. All the same, it was gratifying when people asked his advice. Perhaps they didn't mind him taking an interest, after all.

Joan was a senior nurse. She has never married: 'Always much too busy.' In fact, she has always been very active in all sorts of spheres involving both people and animals (she has five cats). The list of associations she belongs to stretches from Amnesty International to the Cats Protection League via the Anglican Pacifists' Fellowship and the World Wildlife Fund. She is used to being surrounded by dependent creatures, animal and otherwise. She refused to think about retirement, and when someone else mentioned it, Joan treated the idea as if it had no reference to herself at all: 'Fifty is absurdly early to retire.' Her friends said that this was nonsense: she would simply have more time for her cats!

Just before she was due to leave, Joan became ill and had to spend the last month of her working life on sick leave. Her friends discovered that she was a patient on the acute ward of a psychiatric hospital. She told them that she was feeling very ashamed. She couldn't cope. She must be going mad, for nothing made any sense to her any more; nothing had any value, any point. She might as well be dead. The next time they visited her she seemed a little better. She became friendly with one or two of the other patients and involved herself in the life of the ward. In a week or so she was back home again.

It took her some months to recover from the trauma of

separation and loss brought on by having to leave the hospital. She will always feel sad when she remembers what a happy life she had when she worked there. She visits the psychiatric ward most weeks, 'Just to talk to them, you know.' Some of her associations and clubs have local branches which she has been able to join. What with this and keeping an eye on the cats she now finds she isn't half as bored as she expected. She's looking round now for a part-time job: 'Something to do with helping people.'

To summarize, then: although retirement is by no means the same as bereavement (except in certain extreme cases which are fortunately rare), there are nevertheless common elements of grief and loss. The cultural assumption that retirement is harder for men than women 'because a man's job is more important to him', if not more important in itself, still exerts considerable pressure. The overall 'shape' of bereavement – shock, disorganization and reorganization – is frequently reproduced in the experience of retirement simply because it is the shape of all important human changes of direction. There is a real need for pastoral counselling which understands that grief passes through various phases and is able to recognize the presence or absence of significant motifs within someone's reaction to retirement.

A counsellor does not need to be professionally trained to do this. It is essential, however, to be a good listener. If you are having to do a lot of listening, you're working well. Next in importance is not being afraid of emotion, your own or the other person's. You will be trying to help somebody express feelings which they find hard to let through their psychological defences. One such feeling is likely to be anger. This is very important, because some people are particularly frightened of feeling anger about anybody except themselves, where it exists in the form of depression. This is particularly common in retirement because many people object very strongly (and often very rightly, let it be said) to the circumstances under which their own experience of severance took place. Very probably they will find their own feelings unacceptable, and refuse to acknowledge them. The counsellor's task is to bring this hidden anger to the surface and so shift the heavy weight of depression which may be precisely what is holding a particular person back from moving from the first stage of shocked denial into the stage of disorganization. This is the stage of emotional chaos, when psychological restraints have collapsed and people say what they didn't know they meant. This can be particularly painful, both for them and for you; but if you can hang on through this stage, there is a good chance that the person you are helping will find his or her own way of coming to terms with the new state of affairs, in the light both of what has happened *and* of what they *really* feel about it.

This is a brief account of the process of counselling somebody undergoing a significant change in their life and finding it particularly hard to cope. I would certainly recommend that anybody trying to help in this way should read about grief and loss in Murray Parkes or Peter Speck; if they feel that they might be in danger of getting out of their depth, they should urge the person concerned to seek professional help by consulting their doctor. As I suggested earlier, a great deal of help of a psychological kind is provided by the spiritual journey symbolized in a rite of passage: an example of such a rite, designed for somebody passing through retirement, is included at the end of this book (Appendix 2).

Finally, those engaged in counselling people whose lives are in the course of being drastically changed should take care that they don't make things worse by allowing their own anxiety to find expression in urging them to 'pull themselves together'. This may seem obvious; but the fact is that many Christians are deeply upset by depression in other people, believing that it shows lack of faith. 'Rejoice,' they say, and are extremely anxious when the exhorted person turns his or her face to the wall. They need not be so worried. As we have seen, depression is an important factor in real existential change. It is characterized by doubt, in oneself and in God. When it passes, the ability to witness returns, often in a richer and more realistic form, as a sense of having been delivered from the darkness and confusion that only recently prevailed. It is a great shame when Christians act as though they think it is always up to us to heal ourselves, and spend their time nagging when they should be showing solidarity with their fellow Christians in distress.

5. Roles, Social and Personal

Some people are so completely identified with the job they do that they have difficulty telling where it ends and they begin. For people like this their job is really their main role in life, and the reason for any status they may possess as human beings. Sociologically speaking, of course, they are right in associating status with role, for status signifies one's position within a system of related social positions, whereas role denotes one's behaviour when engaged in actions appropriate to one's particular status.

Social psychologists use the word 'role' to mean the characteristics of a particular position within society. It is society that gives you your role, which you share with everyone who does your job. A judge or bus driver, for example, is expected to perform the tasks associated with his or her job regardless of their inclinations: sentencing law-breakers and picking up passengers are their social roles and society expects them to perform them. Roles which are as widely acknowledged as these are often equipped with their own uniforms and jargon. The majority of social roles, however, are much less clearly defined, as well as being more easily assumed and abandoned as their occupier thinks fit. In fact, we all have a repertoire of them, a list of social 'parts' that we are accustomed to playing: son, employee, friend, father, cricket spectator, and so on. It is important to realize that we are not playing these roles in the sense that an actor performs a part in a play. However closely an actor identifies with his or her role, acting always involves a conscious intention to 'be' somebody else: part of being an actor is to be aware that you are taking part in an alternative reality. Social roles, however, are 'played closer to the chest' than this, being an actual aspect of the self. It is your life that is being staged, presented in its interaction with others.

Put it like this. The person I see as myself depends to a considerable degree upon the people among whom I am being it, the social situation in which my life is set. It has been pointed out that the idea of having a personal name combines at least two ways of understanding oneself, as it originates as an interpersonal identification, a mark of status, and becomes a private possession, something we take to ourselves. Identity has always possessed this dual or reflexive nature. It seems that the self has two sides: what *they* call me, and how *I* know me. Standing outside ourselves we see ourselves as others see us. To this extent, identity and role are the same thing, and my reality corresponds to the specifications laid down for me by the parts I play in society. This was the view of the great social psychologist, G.H. Mead.

Later writers have allowed the individual more autonomy. Erving Goffman regards role identity as a co-operative enterprise, in which the role commits the individual to a particular self-understanding when he or she undertakes it, but not before. In fact, Goffman sees a degree of theatrical self-consciousness in the way we play our social roles. He talks about 'role-distance', the technique which allows us to manipulate the role we play so as to exploit the skill we have attained in 'being' a whole range of different selves. For instance, we can play our role with conscious skill in order to make it more convincing, as a preacher takes special care to sound as sincere as possible (this doesn't mean that he isn't sincere, only that he knows how to sound it!); or we can consciously allow ourselves to take less trouble than usual, and enjoy the release of social tension that this sometimes brings with it. 'Despite sociological assumptions, the phenomenon of role-distance demonstrates that we are not the role we play,' says

59

Goffman; he adds that 'what we are remains an open question'.

It seems, then, that despite our need to be aware of social pressure to be a certain kind of person, we are free to choose the roles we want to play, or to play the ones we have to play in the way we want to play them. Another psychologist, George Kelly, built an entire theory of human behaviour on this claim, calling it 'Personal Construct Theory'. It has a lot to teach us about the ways we see ourselves and the roles we play in the drama of living. Kelly turned the tables on the social psychologists who claimed that we are totally dependent on our social position – our family, our school, our job – for the way that we see ourselves. Our view of things, it seems, is always very much *our* view rather than something imposed on us by our environment. Certainly, we are constantly affected by other people, and are emotionally dependent on them to a greater or lesser degree at every moment of our lives. In the first months of life another person is the totality of our universe, a reality from which we cannot distance ourselves or even try to. And when we can, being a separate person is the occasion for relationship and love as we reach out to share life with others. At each crisis of our life the need for sharing presents itself in ways that we had forgotten when life was proceeding smoothly. We remember at such times how beholden we are to what is not ourselves. The world at such times is something that happens to us.

Even so, although we cannot say it belongs to us (not since these first months, anyhow) the fact remains that we do not actually belong to it, in the sense of having no control over it. Things may happen within our sphere of reference, but it is we who make them into events by giving them significance. This is because, whatever happens, we retain the right to interpret it, to tell ourselves exactly what it means so far as we are concerned. We can do this not once, but many times, changing our personal reality each time we construe the situation. Kelly puts it like this:

Each person devises as best he can a structure for making sense of a world of humanity in which he finds himself . . . he makes social predictions on the basis of this construction . . . without such patterned structure it would appear that no man can come to grips with his seething world of people, nor can he establish himself as a psychological entity.

This may seem a far-fetched idea – that the awareness I have of the world I live in, the desk I write at, the room and furniture, the job I must go and do in a few minutes and ought to have done yesterday, owes its particular quality to what I have put into these things and not to some immutable law which I have inherited which lays down how I must regard desks and rooms and jobs. I could quite easily, for instance, prefer doing household tasks to writing books, and have my own perfectly good reasons for my preference. They would be good because they would conform to the way in which I personally valued things, the meaning I had come to read into the actions and relationships of life.

Meaning and value are the two important ideas. The web of meaning is spun according to what has either more or less value. People, ideas, events, things, fall into place according to how important they are and the degree to which they are related to one another in the overall plan of meaning which I am always elaborating for myself: the plan of what matters to me, which of course includes whatever I construe as important to others. At some time (and this is the crucial point) I can change what matters, either in a minor way, and at the lowest degree of importance, deciding to shift the degree of significance I will give to a certain action, thought, attitude; or radically, so that the basis of the way I construe the meaning of reality is changed, and to this extent I will become 'a different person, both to myself and others'. Kelly called this freedom to change our personal worlds 'Constructive Alternativism'. It is the foundation-stone of his philosophy as well as the systematic psychological approach to which this gave rise.

Like many innovators, Kelly uses his own jargon. 'Constructs' are mental tools for ordering the universe. By 'construe' he meant take more or less account of, so that a 'strong' construct implies something which stands out clearly in our minds and is more likely to be taken into account in the plans we make for living, whether these are immediate or long term, than a 'weak' construct, which gives us less to go on. 'Strong' constructs are often abstract. They are the values we live by. Constructs associated with them represent ideas and experiences we really feel at home with; things that fit in with our understanding of life. This feeling of 'rightness' spreads outwards from the most fundamental (or 'superordinate') constructs to the system's edge, the pragmatic ideas and provisional theories we use to make sense of things we are only vaguely interested in or concerned about. All constructs are interconnected, otherwise thinking would be impossible: together they make up an integrated construct system. This is someone's personal view of life. If it is changed in a drastic way the result will be confusion, and the individual concerned will be forced to work hard on a thinking and feeling level to restore some kind of integrity, make some new connections, promote some older, perhaps weaker constructs to a new importance within the total system, so that the balance may be restored – much as a Saturday-afternoon gardener finds a new commitment to gardening once he is away from the office for good. Less far-reaching changes give rise to adjustments that are more minor, hardly affecting the things that are central to the system, although everything leaves its mark somewhere and constitutes a degree of change within the whole.

It is as if each one of us were to have her or his individual mental tool-kit for fixing the things we have to deal with, in the sense of understanding the problems that they represent. For instance, to take the sphere of entertainment: which book shall we read, which play shall we see? One person looks for quality of plot, another for style of writing or acting; one person likes to weep, another would much rather laugh. Each judges merit accordingly. These are all *personal* ways of construing; taken all together, the criteria we consider to be significant reasons for drawing our conclusions are unlikely to be the same as anyone else's. For each of our personal systems some things are important: more dominant, less escapable, than others. Obviously, if we can find out what these things are, and how they relate to the rest of our thinking, we shall have established something very important about ourselves. It may not be possible to change these fundamental criteria of significance. Indeed, we may not want to. On the other hand, we may discover ways of altering their relationships to some of the other things that are important to us. When these 'superordinate constructs' exert an oppressive dominance over the entire system, ways can be found of relieving pressure by reorganizing our attitude towards them. Apart from this, ideas tend to 'tie in' with one another in order to make a common kind of sense. Take, for example, the ideas 'love' and 'friendship'. In some people's construct systems constructs form tight clusters of shared meaning, whereas other people have systems that are loosely organized. Loose systems shift easily because their way of understanding life, and consequently of predicting events, lacks precise definition. Tight systems are harder to modify, and more likely to retain their new shape. If a system is too loosely organized it can be 'tightened up' by what Kelly refers to as 'validation', the process whereby our present state of mind is underlined by the opinions of other people and made capable of real change.

We can see the relevance of Kelly's ideas to the problem of role relinquishment involved in retirement. All that has to be done, it seems, is to learn new mental habits after having first unlearned old ones! Unfortunately, it is rarely as simple as this. Just as one's social role is integral to, and interdependent with, a whole section of society, so a particular way of thinking, feeling, learning and reacting is part of an entire network of complementary reactions. Habitual ways of thinking and feeling, of interpreting the world, are extremely hard to dislodge. As we have seen, they constitute integral parts of systems carefully organized to perform the essential task of predicting what is likely to happen in any eventuality, so that we shall always be able to respond appropriately. This being so, they cannot be dispensed with out of hand, but only replaced by something which will have proved itself capable of performing the same kind of function within our total mental economy. In practical terms this means that the new habits must be learned before the old ones have been abandoned. Indeed, this is the only way it can happen, because the process of learning something new is the main factor in dislodging whatever it was that was there before, the usefulness of which has now come to an end, in its previous form at least.

Habitual ways of perceiving and behaving are extremely hard to dislodge. Psychiatrists have described something that they call the 'Golden Wedding Crisis'. This affects married couples and is very widespread. According to Lawrence Ratna, 'As long as roles are strictly defined – he is out all day working, she is in charge of the home – the relationship is stable and happy. When he retires and starts encroaching on her territory and they begin to spend a lot of time in each other's pockets, hidden conflicts surface and frictions develop.' Patterns like these are not only part of the structure of our understanding, connected to all sorts of major and minor aspects of the way we make sense of life; they themselves possess a certain inalienable attractiveness, the ease and comfort of being us: 'This is the kind of person I am. Doctors (or hospital porters or seaside landladies) are always like this. This is what we always do: I don't know how I'd get on if I didn't.' It's very easy to think like this and go on doing it: 'I'll never change. This is the real me.' Perhaps everybody thinks like this at some time or another. Perhaps we feel it most when we approach retirement. After all, it took us long enough to attain so satisfying an identification of person and role. It seems as though we no sooner really feel at ease in the job than we have to relinquish it! The prospect of having to loose one's moorings and drift away into the unknown makes the place where you have harboured so long particularly precious.

Retirement has caused dislodgement from your core role. Whatever happens now, life will never be the same again! Well, of course it won't be. But then again, it never was. Life is always changing, as in a multitude of small ways, some of them so subtle that you hardly notice them, the relationship between you and your role adjusts to take account of the shifting circumstances of social life. It may be that the kind of thing you have to do doesn't change much, but your attitude to it is affected by adjustments taking place in all sorts of other areas of living. If, by any effort of will, you retained exactly the same ideas, feelings and expectations about your own role, other people's requirements would, over the years, certainly change, thereby affecting the specifications for the proper performance of your role. However much you may hold to the idea that there is no 'relationship' between you and your role; that you *are* your role, so that you will always be a teacher, an undertaker, a deep-sea fisherman, even when so far as you are concerned the job is over, and there is no longer anyone to teach or to bury, no herring to trawl for; however violently you may reject the only role available to you in that particular sphere of life, which is that of ex-teacher, former undertaker, retired seadog, claiming that you will always be the person you always were, that times may change but you remain the same – the fact is that no job has that kind of hold over anybody, even if we should want it to. At present we have no idea of ourselves as *not* a teacher, fisherman, civil servant, but that can be changed. So long as we are human we can choose our role, because our role is the terms of our relationship with other people. It may involve professional qualifications, the payment of wages, manual skill, even union membership, but basically it is an attitude of mind, and can therefore be changed.

In fact, in most people's construct systems (the repertoire of personal judgements which tell us what the world

65

is like and what to expect from it) other things exercise higher authority than jobs. When they are asked to say what is most important to them, people who don't say 'God' say 'My family'. It is true that even those who do not particularly like their jobs tend to rate employment high, because it is the thing that seems to guarantee social identity. On the other hand, it rarely manages to overtop 'health' or even 'friendship'. Any event which takes place in our lives that does not lead us to question these super-ordinate considerations is a relatively unimportant one; by which I mean that the real, fundamental role, the way that she or he interprets life itself, is not threatened by it. These are the factors which need to be strengthened and encouraged, if 'lower-level' expectations are reversed by significant changes in the circumstances affecting our-selves, such as when we retire from work. We have seen that people organize their expectations of the world in order to take account of the things that happen to them by relating them to whatever has taken place. At whatever 'level of expectation' changes occur, the result will be a degree of disorientation and distress. The higher the value affected – if, for instance, a firmly held belief in friendship were to be seriously threatened by evidence of extreme personal treachery – the greater the confusion and uncer-tainty experienced with regard to less important and inte-gral parts of the system, all of which depend on the exist-ence, in an unchallenged state, of these higher ideas. For instance, if I can't trust my oldest friend, I'm not sure I can give my support to 'free' discussion after the Evening Service with people I don't know.

Considerations of personality and social circumstances will cause different people to register the significance of retirement at different levels in their construct systems. The circumstances of retirement will be different for each, so that each will see it as a different kind of event, more or less expected, more or less welcome, more or less dis-turbing. It is unlikely, however, that there will be a perfect fit between the event which is envisaged, and conse-quently prepared for, and the one that actually occurs. If, however, there is part of the person's construct system that would have lent itself to a better way of coming to terms with the event as it really happened; if, for instance, beside my expectations of carrying on working until retirement age I also have well-developed ideas about the importance of behaving in ways that promote the company's best interests, I may be relieved of some of the distress I would otherwise have felt at being made to take early retirement 'for the good of the firm'. Notice, however, that the mitigating idea is already present. It is not something invented by the company to soften the blow: 'You know you've always said that if it came to the push. . . .' I may or may not have said it; the fact is that I must really have meant it if it is going to do me any good now. One of the tasks of construct psychology is to help people find out the whole range of what they *really mean*, so that they can use it to adapt to the challenge of life, and particularly to things that are unforeseen. What they *really mean* may provide backing for a whole range of alternative ways of adapting to life, a whole range of roles.

Maurice is an Anglican priest, vicar of a small country parish several miles from the nearest town. He has held the incumbency for round about ten years, the usual length of time for him to stay in one part of the country. The time has come for him to make another move, only this time he is going into retirement and not to another new parish. For the last few years, he has been spending part of his holidays, and any free time he was willing to allow himself, at a cottage situated on the East Anglican coast, near to his first parish, in fact. It is a very nice cottage, only five minutes' walk from the sea and on a bus route to the nearby town (Maurice doesn't drive). He has several old friends in the neighbourhood and is always made very welcome when he visits them. In addition, the local rector is an old acquaintance and arrangements have been made for Maurice to act as a semi-official curate (unpaid) helping with services in the church from time to time, so that he won't feel completely out of touch. It will be different from the life he has known as an active parish priest but it will be interesting in its own way, and very restful. What Maurice needs, above all, is a rest. These last few years have been spent on the verge of a breakdown. Maurice's friends, and his doctor, are not all that sanguine of his chances of ever relaxing and enjoying his retirement.

In fact, Maurice rarely relaxes. It is, and always has been, very important to him to be not merely an active parish priest but a super-active one. 'I would like people to say about me that I was totally wedded to the parish,' he likes to say. He has said it about each one of the four parishes where he has been vicar, and he always means it. He is not, in fact, married; a Freudian might say there is an element of sexual sublimation in his devotion to his work. Maurice chose to enter the priesthood because he believed that he would find, in God's service, the special grace needed to overcome homosexual tendencies which he recognized in himself. His plan worked only too well; during the last forty years he has remained passionately faithful to his first love, so that you could say he is totally involved in his chosen calling, having devoted all his emotional life to the job of being as good a parish priest as possible.

The trouble is that the time has now come for him to relinquish at least part of his role, and be just a priest, not a parish one. This is not an easy thing for an ex-vicar to do. Generally speaking, the Anglican Church tends to neglect its unbeneficed clergy, leaving them to lead shadowy existences in someone else's parish, having spiritual authority without any official ways of exercising it – not *here*, at any rate! Maurice feels as if he has nowhere to go where he can be himself. He is living in the cottage, but he can't settle there. He feels as if he is on holiday and wants to get back to reality. None of his friends is able to help him, and he just refuses to take part in the parish church services as a priest. He will go to church but not officiate in any way. Soon, he says, he will probably stop going at all.

That was the situation some weeks ago. I'm glad to say that since then the situation has improved. Maurice's GP, alarmed by the course things were taking, persuaded him to see a clinical psychologist, and she seems to have been of some help to him. One of the things she asked him to do was to write down a short description of himself, saying what kind of things he liked and disliked, what interested him, what upset him – what sort of a person did he think he was? Was he someone he would like to know? Why? Why not? She was very serious about all this; what's more, she took him very seriously, obviously believing all that he said about himself. Then she got him to write a short character sketch of himself as he would like to be, and they spent some time discussing the differ- ences. Maurice had been instructed to say what he really felt not what he felt he ought to feel, and that in itself was a considerable help because it allowed him to think more clearly about his situation and to identify what it was that was really important to him in his life, as a priest and as a human being. Next time he saw her they worked out a kind of compromise plan; he would include some of the features from the second account ('Myself as I would like to be') in a third description, 'Myself as I might pos- sibly manage to be'. This took a good deal of thinking and praying about. Maurice was caught between two opposing impulses: on the one hand he wanted to do well and exalt the spirit at the flesh's expense. On the other he had serious doubts as to whether he could change in any way at all. The kind of change envisaged was in the direction of greater realism; Maurice knew very well that he had somehow to come to terms with the differences between his old way of life and the new situation. He was so confounded by the negative aspects of the change, the things he would no longer be able to do, that he had refused to think practically about anything connected with retirement. But he had never thought of himself as a prac- tical person, in any case; practical, down-to-earth, able to live from day to day, these were some of the things he aimed at being. In painstakingly assimilable form they were all included in the new description. Maurice took it away with him and consulted it from time to time. He took it very seriously. It was, after all, his own blueprint. Giving it reality became his project.

Being a priest had made Maurice very lazy. Certainly, he had had to work very hard indeed, but he very rarely exercised his full responsibilities as a human being. He very rarely made decisions which affected his own way of life. The priesthood tends to be a totalitarian role, one which occupies one's entire waking existence, in which there is, to use Goffman's phrase, no 'back-stage' activity, nothing to provide a welcome release from one's public face. In Maurice's construct system, directly under 'God' (or more accurately 'God/Christ/Spirit') were 'my priesthood' and 'my responsibility to the parish'. Anything that related, in any way, to these three ideas made him feel inspired and happy at the same time. As most of the things he came into contact with were directly concerned with them, or at least could be made to appear so, his daily life was untroubled by the necessity to make personal decisions which might disturb his emotional equilibrium. Maurice knew what to think, because he firmly knew how to believe. Within its limits his life possessed integrity, although it was scarcely adult.

Maurice knew this and described himself in this way to the clinical psychologist (using the third person in order to be as objective as possible): 'Maurice is a two-dimensional man. For twenty years he has only been half alive. This half has worked very hard, really done its best. It has had some good friends, real people living real lives. I don't know what's happened to the other half. Perhaps I would be able to help him if it really existed.' In the second account of himself, the 'ideal self', this unseen half, appeared again. This time, however, it had gained flesh: 'Maurice is a well-rounded personality, with a private as well as a public self. These two selves are not separate in any way – neither can exist without the other. It is what is discovered privately about what life means that lends wisdom to the public self; it is sharing in other people's lives that gives courage to the private self. Both are part of Maurice's priesthood.'

By dividing himself up like this Maruice has pointed the way to envisaging a much better balance on his third, final, self-portrait: 'In a sense, Maurice knows who he is, and who he has been during the years of his ministry. In a sense he doesn't know, any more than any of us know, who the real Maurice is. Now he is in a position to find out. He will try to use the past as a jumping-off ground for the future. There's a lot of the past, and it's all valuable. It is the future, however, where life is, and that's where Maurice is going.'

At the age of sixty-five, Maurice is learning to manage a role instead of allowing the role to manage him. It doesn't matter how worthy and exalted a role is, if it detracts from the humanity of the man or woman who possesses it, it never functions to the best advantage. Whatever the role may be, its effect depends on the way in which it is managed in order to convince people that your social role is in fact what you claim it is. You must be conscious of what you are doing and of the effect it is having; in order to avoid being swallowed up by your own performance, you must be conscious that it is *you* who are doing it. You are functioning as yourself. There must always be a *me* to choose between various roles. This is quite different from the suspension of disbelief involved in acting. Effective role-management requires developing a strong sense of the self, in order that the role may be used as it should be; that is, as the personalized form of a social function. The purpose here is not to disguise a human being, but to draw attention to a human being's particular characteristics, among which may be knowledge, skill, understanding, all of which depend first and foremost on his or her underlying humanity.

Maurice had particular difficulty with his role as a clergyman. It must never be forgotten that at a deeper level than role-involvement, a distinction must be drawn between those who find personal fulfilment and satisfaction in their job and try to reproduce this in retirement, and those who are unsatisfied by what they have done in the past, either by the job itself or by their own showing

71

in it, and are still searching. The latter see retirement as a welcome change of direction, the opportunity to continue their search further. Perhaps, as with Maurice, there are usually elements of both. No two situations can ever be exactly alike. In many cases a compromise must somehow be arrived at. It is a fortunate man or woman who has the opportunity to work through the issues involved in the way that Maurice did.

The kind of approach used in this instance is quite common nowadays. It is called the 'narrative approach', and is based on the idea that since our view of ourselves falls naturally into the story-form, we may be able to change the former by adopting a different version of the latter. In fact, telling your own story, taking the trouble to write it down and read it to someone else, does have a very definite effect on the way you think of yourself. People who do it report that they have a firmer grip on themselves. Their construct system is drawn together by asserting the ideas, values and events that de-limit it. Ideas and events become more closely associated, and we become more closely identified with our story in the process of making it our own in this conscious, creative way. Of course, there are elements in it that we can stress, elements we can play down. In this way we can change it, using material already present in it, explicitly or implicitly. Because it is our story, in reshaping it like this, we potentially reshape ourselves, giving our aspirations a particular location. As James Hillman says, 'I need to remember my stories, not because I need to find out about myself, but because I need to found myself in a story I can hold to be "mine".' This may not be historically accurate, but in a real sense it is authentically mine: it represents me. Stories are about people.

This story is still going on. We are not at the end of this particular episode yet. Maurice is still not happy about what is going on – not as happy as when life was simple and he had his parish to look after. There is no doubt that things are beginning to improve, however, now he has the time and inclination to look where he's going. This way he will, through God's grace, eventually discover who he is.

6. Work

'Work' and 'role' belong together. We feel that we *are* what we *do*. Work is central to our life as human beings. Eric Erikson explains how this occurs from the point of view of our growth and psychological development:

> Its origin coincides with the period in a child's life when the desire to manipulate people, which characterized the first years of infancy – once it had become possible to distinguish the presence of other people as existing apart from the self – is turned towards the inorganic environment. . . . He has experienced a sense of finality regarding the fact that there is no workable future within the womb of his family, and thus becomes ready to apply himself to given skills and tasks. . . . He develops a sense of industry – i.e. he adjusts himself to the inorganic laws of the tool world. . . . To bring a productive situation to completion is an aim which gradually supersedes the whims and wishes of play.

In psychoanalytic terms, work is a division of the pleasure principle; a way of using things instead of people as instruments of self-gratification. Thus Marcuse talks about 'the transformation of the pleasure principle into the performance principle'. Others have said quite simply that work is the highest form of pleasure, and people should not be deprived of it simply because they are old. Whether or not we agree with this, it certainly throws light on the pleasure we get from work that we like doing – and the frustration we feel when our work doesn't respond to all our efforts to make it yield 'job satisfaction'.

When we say that work is vitally necessary to the life

of human beings, we mean much more than that society depends on the production of food, housing, transport, communication media, and so on. We need to work in order to satisfy our material needs – at least, most of us do. Just as importantly, however, we need to work for the satisfaction of other needs, which are social and psychological and spiritual in nature, and without which we do not feel we are really genuinely alive. Paid employment is not the only way in which such demands can be met, but it is one way. It fulfils our need to undertake obligations within society, to be regarded as important and significant people, to feel important and significant ourselves. There are at least two ways in which work makes us feel personally worthwhile: when we find satisfaction in the work itself, or in the way we do it, and when the actual work provides the structure and setting for relationships and social ties around which our view of life is organized. Thus NHS workers, anxious about their jobs and the prospect of redundancy, draw closer together in order to give one another support in time of trial: 'We do get lonely and depressed, but at least we've got each other to bounce things off against.' Relationships at work are not the only ones we have, but they are very important to us all the same. We may not even consider them to be key relationships. In a study of family, gender and retirement, Ofra Anderson and a team of Israeli psychologists came to the conclusion that 'marriage and the proximity of children may compensate for some of the void created by retirement, but the void is still there and the losses do not necessarily fade away'; and this was in connection with Jewish families! Lawrence Ratna, in what he calls 'Retirement Arrest Syndrome', says that it is 'because life seems to come to a full stop after retirement. Where once people have been active and outgoing, following retirement they become withdrawn, inactive and depressed.' An examination of most working people's personal construct systems reveals that the extent to which they interpret life in terms of what happens at work is greater than might be expected. We may like to forget the office, the shop-floor, or the classroom when we get home, but these places are very important to us, and what we see on television during the evening we are likely to construe in terms of what has happened to us during the day.

All the same, the statement that 'work is central to our experience' needs qualification, particularly from a sociological point of view. Less than half the population of the United Kingdom is classified as 'gainfully employed'. In 1962 the average number of hours worked each week, overtime included, was 47.1, which means that less than half of a person's waking hours were spent at work. The proportion is certainly less today than it was then. The point is that the time spent working is so extremely important, economically, socially and cognitively: that is, from the point of view of the way we make sense of ourselves and the world we live in. We have seen how work is crucial as the giver of identity and status: 'What is she?' 'She is a midwife.' We know what kind of a job she does, certainly: what is more important, we know how to regard her *as a person doing this particular job*. It is as if she and her job merged in order to fit in with our expectations. Her job gives us a way of relating to her, because it fits specifications we already possess. Although we have never met her, she is not entirely a stranger; we have, as actors say of the characters in plays, a line on her.

Work of some kind or another would appear to be essential. Even when it is unpaid, and has no economic significance, it can serve the purpose of bringing us into some kind of interaction with other people, thus helping us to be fully human. Even solitary work occupies our actual minds and regulates our shapeless days. More and more people do more than one job; women who 'go out to work' spend much of their adult lives doing two jobs. Asked to say what retirement felt like, an engineer said, 'The trouble is that you can't really prepare for it.' Urged to be more explicit he said, 'It's very difficult to foretell what the effect of having no structured work will be like. What you don't expect is the absence of stimulation, the sheer, crushing boredom.' Certainly, not everybody will experience this to anything like this extent. On the other hand, the lack of recognizable shape in one's day-to-day living is a factor many retired people remark on: 'Even if you're expecting it, it's like coming to the edge of a precipice. Maybe you'll find you can walk on air. Maybe you'll find you can't. Or perhaps there'll be parachutes' (actor); 'I've worked for forty years because I've had to. What'll it be like, when I don't have to?' (shop-keeper).

The last statement, coming from the proprietor of an ironmonger's shop that had survived the DIY revolution, gets near to the heart of the problem. People are ambivalent about work. Though they may not like it, they will still cling to it. I suggest that this is because it serves the indispensable function of limiting human freedom while shouldering the responsibility for doing so. Work answers the question 'What shall I do next?' in ways that can be construed as not being my fault. It lets us off the hook with regard to the question about what we should be doing with our lives. It is the Aunt Sally provided for us by the facts of economic existence. Sociologists have drawn attention to the way that 'work restricts our liberty to follow our own personal aims and intentions'. Herbert Marcuse, for example, points out that 'the realm of necessity, of labor, is one of unfreedom because the human existence in this realm is determined by objectives and functions that are not its own and that do no allow the free play of human faculties and desires'. What Marcuse does not say, however, is that this provision of 'objectives and functions' is much appreciated by those of us who are not always sure what to be and how to be it. There seems to be no problem, for most of us, in identifying with these ready-made ideas and patterns of action which are always culturally as well as economically rewarded, and soon become a part of our own personal lives, to be loved and hated just as they would have been if we had thought them up for ourselves. To this extent, perhaps, we suffer from what Marx called 'alienation': we are excluded from choice as to how our own work may contribute to the public good, and open to exploitation by people in a position to use our labour for their own ends. Some of us may regret this more than others, however.

For most people, perhaps, the most important thing about work is that it keeps one occupied and provides the money needed in order to survive 'in the manner to which you have been accustomed'. Many, if not most, would need to be assured that their labour was not being used to further projects of which, on ethical or religious grounds, they did not approve. Because work is primarily an expression of human freedom, human beings must bear the responsibility for the way they use the freedom given them. Emil Brunner, one of the greatest moral theologians of this century, makes a good deal of this point. On the other hand, as many writers have pointed out, there is a marked tendency for work to be self-validating so that it does not depend entirely on its outcome for ethical justification. It is good simply to work.

This would certainly seem to be the biblical view. Unlike the Ancient Greeks, who preferred to leave all kinds of manual labour to slaves, the Hebrews saw work as a divine obligation, binding on the whole community: 'Six days shalt thou labour and do all thy work' (Exodus 20:9). This attitude is carried over into New Testament times, when rabbis were expected to learn a trade as their main source of income (such as Paul and Aquila, Acts 18:3, both tent-makers). St Paul was quite definite about the universal need to work, pronouncing to the effect that 'if any will not work, neither let him eat'. When the Lord came again the situation might be different. For the time being, however, Christians continued to work for the common good, although their motivation was love, not law.

It is sometimes claimed that the Bible teaches us that work is God's way of punishing humanity for the disobedience of Adam and Eve in the Garden of Eden. In fact, Adam was placed in the garden 'to dress it and to keep it', having been created in the first place in order to 'replenish the earth and subdue it: and have dominion

. . . over every living thing' (Genesis 2:15, 1:28). Work is the normal, healthy, satisfactory way for men and women to occupy themselves: 'Man goeth forth unto his work and to his labour until the evening' (Psalms 104:23). Skill and craftsmanship are part of the wisdom Yahweh bestows as a gift on his creation (Exodus 35:30–36:2). This is always the divine intention. It is humanity that has caused work to become, or to become seen as, a punishment or a curse. Work is part of the natural order which mankind's sin has corrupted. The first part of Genesis clearly demonstrates how the whole field of work, which should be the setting for loving co-operation, has been torn apart by selfishness, rivalry and fratricidal quarrelling (see Genesis 4); indeed, the very ground itself seems to have caught mankind's infection, for it is full of thorns and thistles (Genesis 3:18).

Thus the Genesis story clearly implies that all the things which make work a hardship rather than a pleasure are the direct effect of human rebellion against God. The result of our 'primal' sin is that the very thing which should have been both congenial and enjoyable has become a burden to be born out of sheer obedience to authority. Work itself was never intended to be a punishment; the punishment subsists in the penal transformation of our relationship with work. The punishment is not work, but our attitude towards work. In the words of Genesis 3:17, 'cursed is the ground for thy sake; in sorrow shall thou eat of it all the days of thy life'.

But the Bible speaks of grace, as well as of law; and the way to re-establish work as the source of satisfaction and self-expression it was meant to be is to be reconciled to God. In the life of a carpenter, God's intention in the creation of the world is totally fulfilled. In Alan Richardson's words, 'It is of the deepest significance for our Christian doctrine of work that God, when for the sake of our salvation he most wonderfully and humbly chose to be made man, was incarnate in a village carpenter and not in a king or statesman or general or philosopher.' He goes on to say that, 'This was the only fitting image for the God whom the biblical tradition had all along represented as himself a worker: "In six days the Lord God made heaven and earth, and on the seventh day rested from his work." ' For Christians work has a special significance as, in a sense, they become more Christlike as their joy in creativity increases. In our work, when it is carried out for God's greater glory, we share his lordship of creation; we really are God's fellow workers (1 Thessalonians 3:2)

Until the Reformation, work was considered to be an important aspect of our relationship with God, but definitely not the most important one. A change was at hand, however. Luther and Calvin concluded that a person's daily work was the proper sphere in which God was to be worshipped. Public and private were no longer to be kept apart from each other. In a sense it can be said that, for Protestant Christians, Luther redefined work, although his redefinition has been widely misunderstood. 'Work' and 'works' were not to be confused. The former should be the spiritual expression of our deliverance from the latter. Our work is an expression of the divine bounty within us, which we have received simply because we have not tried to earn it. In post-Reformation writing, however, there is a strong suggestion that it is morally reprehensible not to work: 'What', asks Louis Bourdaloue, 'is the disorder of an idle life? It is, replies St Ambrose, in its true meaning a second rebellion of the creature against God.' Commenting on this attitude, Michel Foucault says that unemployment represents a breach of 'the great ethical pact of human existence'.

Describing the attitude of the Calvinistic Puritans to work, Tawney writes that, 'since conduct and action, though availing nothing to attain the free gift of salvation, are a proof that the gift has been accorded, *what is rejected as a means is resumed as a consequence*, and the Puritan flings himself into practical activities with the daemonic energy of one who, all doubts allayed, is conscious that he is a sealed and chosen vessel'. Tawney is quick to point out that the Puritan spirit made a tremendous contribution to political freedom, and consequently to social progress. The democratic ideal, which is largely founded on the self-confidence and courage of individuals, has always had difficulty in finding expression in a nation where class privilege has for centuries been a fact of public life so well established as to be either ignored or taken for granted: 'democracy owes more to Nonconformity than to any other single movement'. The intense privacy of Puritan religious awareness had the paradoxical effect of making religion public by weaving it into the fabric of ordinary life to an extent that had never happened before. As Max Weber says, 'the Puritan could demonstrate his religious merit precisely in his economic activity' – a feat that until then nobody had managed to perform with anything like the same success.

Unfortunately for successive generations this notable achievement in the direction of freedom and self-expression proceeded from what Weber calls the 'distinctively ascetic motivation characteristic of Puritans'. The obligation to treat life and work in a spirit of celebration characteristic of Lutheranism was absent from Puritanism. The sanctification of commerce gave work a distinctively religious value, thereby rendering it inescapably judgemental. Work became something one did even when one didn't need to, in order to punish oneself. In Max Weber's words, 'the spirit of religious asceticism . . . has escaped from the cage [of the medieval monasteries] . . . and the idea of duty in one's calling prowls about in our lives like the ghost of dead religious beliefs'. Harvey Cox puts it equally dramatically: 'For the man who has left behind the tribal cults but has not yet reached the stage of full secularity, the job has become a spiritual devotion.' And, we might add, a particularly harsh one, too. Generations of British people have associated work with hard labour (or at least with the absence of any kind of enjoyment) and have laid the blame for their attitude, explicitly or implicitly, on God. The prevailing attitude is that if you enjoy it, it isn't work. Many people hold that work is unpleasant by definition.

Laurence used to argue about this in the pub. 'It's what

81

This is a caricature of Puritanism! Why on earth is Weber still built an expect on it?

work *means*,' he said. 'If you have a job you enjoy, you're being paid for not working. This is just one of those facts of life you have to put up with,' he said. 'Work is what you do in order to earn money to enjoy yourself. *You* don't enjoy working,' he said, 'I've seen you. You look worse than me sometimes.' It was pointed out to him that one at least tried to like one's job, and even succeeded quite often, but it was no good. One might as well try to convince him of a liking for toothache.

Laurence was the only son of the owner of a factory which made electrical components. The business had grown rapidly over the last twenty or thirty years, but when Laurence was a boy it was still quite small. Sometimes, during his school holidays, his father used to take him round the workshop. Laurence enjoyed this; it made him feel grown up, and he liked talking to the men and women who were working there. They were so much easier to talk to than the other adults in his life, who seemed to spend all the time talking about him, never themselves. A lonely boy, with parents who asked a lot in the way of obedience and respect but when it came to expressing feelings of appreciation and love, 'didn't go in for that sort of thing'. Laurence appreciated the opportunity to spend a day in his father's company because it made him feel particularly close to the person he admired more than any other in the entire world.

The business of making electrical components didn't interest him half so much, however ('You don't complain about the money, though, do you?' said his father). Laurence had other preoccupations. All through his childhood he had been deeply attracted to the study of social history. (Political history, the movement of armies and the fortunes of dynasties, did not concern him, except in so far as these things affected the lives of ordinary people.) He was bitterly disappointed, therefore, when his father suggested that he should join the company in a rather humble clerical position when he left school. Laurence had done well enough in his Higher School Certificate to justify applying for a place at university, but when he spoke to his father about his ambition to become a social historian his father laughed at him and told him that jobs like that were for clever people. Laurence, he said, was average, certainly not brilliant. There really wasn't any point in his going to university – especially not when he was needed in the family business. He was exceedingly lucky, he said, to have a job to go right into. He (Laurence's father) had not been half so fortunate; when *he* left school the business consisted of a lean-to shed, and so on and so forth.

Immediately upon leaving school Laurence had to do National Service, serving as a lance-corporal in the Royal Corps of Signals. After the initial culture shock, he settled down to two years of almost unrelieved boredom, along with the rest of his generation. In after years, Laurence used to say that he did not regret the time he spent in the Army: 'I met a lot of ordinary folk and learned a bit about life.' When he left he went straight into making electrical components without complaining. His mother had died during his absence, and he felt that his father needed all the support he could get. Besides, his father was probably right.

As a matter of fact, Laurence turned out to be quite a successful businessman. The company grew and flourished, as he steered it skilfully first into the electronics field, then into miniaturized components and, finally, computers. Laurence was equally fortunate in his personal life, falling in love with and marrying the daughter of a successful manufacturer for whom Laurence's firm did contract work. The next thirty years were particularly happy ones: Laurence was respected by his business colleagues and competitors and liked (in some cases even loved) by his workforce. Working in industry had not changed him. He was still, first and foremost, a man who was interested in people. When his local Council of Churches discussed the possibility of setting up a counselling service, it was Laurence who took the idea up, organizing it and taking his place on the rota of counsellors. He was a Samaritan for many years. All this time he and his wife were busy bringing up their own family, and doing so with more success than they, the parents that is, would admit.

Altogether, an ordinary kind of story. When disaster came it was an ordinary kind of calamity; not a fatal illness, a crippling bereavement, or death by accident. This was a subtler blow, what might be called a commercial stab-in-the-back. Laurence's company, the family firm, although changed out of recognition by take-overs and rationalizations, decided that they could no longer afford a managing director earning as much as he did, and resolved to substitute someone younger (and consequently not so expensive). Suddenly, without warning, Laurence received what is usually called the 'golden handshake'. He was fifty-eight years old.

It was a great shock. Laurence felt betrayed by his own company. Who, he wondered, was behind this? There hadn't been any indication that such a thing might happen. He was also shocked and disgusted by the way that he had been told about it – he had been asked to attend a discussion about the possibility of 'early retirement' after the decision to get rid of him had already been taken by the board. Most of all, however, he felt thwarted and frustrated. The company was his life's work. Why couldn't he see it through until he was old enough to retire?

Not that he had ever liked working for it very much. The cut and thrust of business was alien to his temperament. It was his ability to get on with people that had made him effective as a manager. For several months Laurence sat around at home, too shocked to do anything at all. Then he began to search the newspaper for jobs. Discouraged by this, he became more and more depressed. Although he really knew very well that what had happened was financial rather than personal, he took it very personally indeed. It seemed to him he had been 'chucked on the rubbish heap' by the people to whom, at considerable expense of spirit, he had devoted his entire working life. Except that it wasn't 'entire'! The family doctor recommended a short stay in a psychiatric hospital. Laurence refused to take his advice, but the idea frightened him into applying for the next job that came along, which was helping to run a small private charity for people with drink problems.

Laurence's experience as an amateur counsellor as well as his administrative skill won him the job. He turned out to be ideally suited for this kind of work. All his life he had enjoyed working with people in an atmosphere of honesty and mutual respect. He felt that, until now, working as he was in the always competitive and often deceitful world of commerce and industry, he had never had the chance to be his real self. For the first time in his life he was really enjoying his work.

Not for long, however. In two years a job came up in the computer industry, the world that Laurence knew best. Laurence applied for it and got it. It was a very good job, bringing in almost as much money as the one he had lost. It was not the money that decided him, however: the reason he swapped jobs was a purely personal one. He liked his counselling job too much. It was as simple as that. He was good at it, it suited him, he enjoyed it and it didn't seem like work. He had undertaken to work 'in the business' all his working life, until retirement came, and even though he didn't like this job so much, that is what he would do. After all, you aren't supposed to like work, are you? That's why it's *work*. It was what his father had always said, and Laurence said it too.

Certainly, there are psychological reasons here concerning Laurence's relationship with his father: his desire to please the person he admired so much and had never managed to please while he was alive (the old man died ten years before Laurence was forcibly 'retired'). There are also psychological factors regarding our relationship to work itself, any kind of work. Our relationship to the work we do, the routines and procedures which gradually invade our lives, changing our construction of the world and our own place in it, affecting the way we 'live and move and have our being' – this relationship is something much more global than the 'learned behaviour' described

85

by psychologists. In a sense it is *where you live*, a world that balances the world of your home life, that includes and is included by it, so that the two are distinguishable but not separable. Work is a place where you have always been, where you do things you've always done – or at least it seems like this. It is part of the web of being in which you are caught, and to which you cling for dear life. How much these feelings are affected by, and contribute to, a cultural definition of work which regards it as the direct expression of our duty to God, it is impossible to say.

What can and must be said is that if this is religious behaviour, it certainly does not seem to be the kind that the Christian Church should be sponsoring. It savours too much of idolatry if not of masochism. Free men and women ought not to be so fatally fascinated by the way in which they earn their bread as to choose jobs that they do not like doing, *because* they don't like doing them. This sounds more like the behaviour of slaves. For work to become holy it must be made to conform to the image of love. The business ethics with which we are familiar, and which affect our lives in so many ways, have a long way to go. In fact, they show no inclination to move in that direction. Love does not figure in any scale of business values that I have heard about; this being the case, we should not expect to be made holy by commerce.

To be fair, most people don't. Quite a few, however, Laurence included, hope to be holy in spite of it; their witness to love will be literally *in spite of* the selfishness that commerce proclaims as a virtue, perhaps the highest one of all. Many Christian businessmen and -women profess this intention; and because it is a very difficult one to sustain (as difficult as trying to serve two masters at the same time) allow the workplace to become a place of guilt, shame at the failure of their good intentions. The god of industry and commerce may all too easily show himself in such circumstances under the guise of an avenger, which is why we treat him with a respect not unmixed with loathing: avengers have to be placated.

Either business ethics have changed since Calvin's time, or the Puritans were misguided in their attempts to praise God in the language of profit and loss. Certainly, fewer people appear to be trying to live life according to one set of rules than in the seventeenth century. The usual tendency nowadays is to treat life and work as if they had little to do with each other, 'religion', above all, having no place in the world of business – that ultra-serious 'real' world of commercial mythology where 'that's *business*' puts an end to all argument. One thing is for certain. The Church must be quite definite in its proclamation that work is not holiness, any more than 'works' are. Only the Gospel news about the primal overarching importance of the totally unearned can exorcise the demon that has crept into our ordinary daily routines and reversed the God-given order, transforming the thing that should be sancti-fied by men and women into the presence whereby they receive sanctification. Of course, it is possible for Christ-ians to work in a competitive world without losing their integrity: consciences may be obeyed, even in business. What is really dangerous, for the peace of mind of a Christ-ian, is the suggestion that he or she can be compromised by what for him or her can never be more than a set of procedures posing as an ethic, something which has no authority over the law of love. Of course, there will be times when we fail to keep that law and find ourselves cutting corners and turning blind eyes in order to secure our interests at others' expense. There may even be times when we do worse things, so that we believe ourselves to be fatally compromised. Even so, God's forgiving love outweighs these things, which certainly cannot be said about the divinity we ascribe to labour. We must not allow our own confusion about where the real authority lies to rule our attitude to work so that it is always a curse, never a blessing. Retirement, which gives us an opportunity to revise some of our opinions about life, may also help us to see work in a slightly different light.

All the same, giving up a job one has been doing for a long time, or making a final break in a long succession of

87

jobs, is a statement about life of a particular significance, one that is underlined by our awareness of the chronic presence of death. Each ending in life reminds us of the ending of all human life. This is certainly true of each of the aspects of retirement we have been considering. Giving up hard-earned authority, laying down a familiar and highly personalized role, passing through a life crisis which alters the terms on which one lives one's life and, finally, giving up one's life's work – all these symbolize dying. They register in our unconscious minds in order to make retirement a staging-post of great significance on our journey towards the grave, surfacing in the way we commonly talk about such things, the metaphors we so often use – phrases like 'the end of the line', 'one step nearer the edge', 'over the hill'. Phrases like these are ominous and depressing, pessimistic ways of looking at life. Surely there is more to retirement than this for Christians?

Well, yes. For one thing, Christians are beginning to look at the world in a new way. 'Creation Theology' concentrates on the physical universe as the setting, and to some extent the source, of human righteousness, rather than as some kind of immense factory to be utilized by human beings as a way of atoning for sin. The Creation represents God's love, which takes precedence over our selfishness and disobedience; for millennia it proclaimed his glory, long before men and women arrived on the scene. To enjoy it, to be renewed by it, is a more authentically Christian thing than to find ways of using it as a stick to beat oneself (and other people) with in order to demonstrate one's ability to suffer in ways that are pleasing to God. With the Resurrection and Ascension of Christ, the universe is restored to its original glory; to accept the holiness of creation is to realize one's own restoration. The Centre for Creation Spirituality, based at St James's Church, Piccadilly, London, reminds us that

> Each human being is a Royal Person who can choose to befriend the darkness, delight in passion, and find fulfilment in making

their own contribution to the Cosmic Order, rather than being a miserable sinner for whom darkness is evil, passion is dangerous and punishment is feared. Anxiety over personal righteousness, perfection and individual salvation are overtaken by justice, wholeness, and compassion for all, and the exclusive confrontation of 'either/or' gives way to the inclusive psychology of 'both . . . and'.

Surely, if this kind of teaching begins to be heard in our cathedrals and churches, we may expect the incidence of psychosomatic illness and stress-induced conditions to decline, as we become 'co-workers with God in an unfolding creation process'.

7. Redundancy

During the time that I have been writing this book I have become aware that the things it says apply to more people than I thought they did. In particular, the problem of redundancy has increased greatly during the last few years, so that very many people now find themselves out of work who never expected to do so. I emphasize this because of the difference in the way someone who is used to having a succession of short-time jobs – a builder, a 'temp', or an actor – looks at their work, and the attitude of mind associated with the traditional 'career' in a business, trade or profession. To lose one's job in such circumstances means much more than simply having to adjust to a reduction in income. It means a radical change in one's way of looking at oneself and one's world. It means an adjustment in 'frame', the way in which we make sense of what is happening to us, the balanced picture of the kind of thing we feel we can expect from life. A great number of people have had their anticipations of the future proved false, so that life has lost its balance: 'I found myself thrashing about trying to find some kind of foothold.' As we have seen, this is the pattern of all radical human change. After a time the old connections drop away and new ones begin to form. Indeed, it would be impossible to grow and develop as people without such experiences, although that doesn't make them easier to bear for those who are personally affected.

Nowadays more and more are personally affected. Those who are in secure jobs no longer feel secure about them. After all, why should they? These things tend to happen suddenly when you least expect it. Everybody has at least one friend who, trustingly opening their breakfast-time mail, has found themselves to be redundant. As the number of unemployed people rise, so the numbers of people who fall under the shadow of unemployment, whose lives are affected by this pervasive uncertainty about the future, continues to increase. Statistics are available for the first but not the second. In a way their plight is worse, because although they are still paid and occupied as they always were, they have no way of knowing how much longer this will go on; what was once the firm basis for their intentions is now a network of suppositions, useless when it comes to making decisions in the present or laying down plans for the future: 'One can only hope for the best, and try not to dwell on the plans we had.' Once the event has taken place, the nature of the anxiety changes. There is a tendency for the time-scale to contract. We no longer reach out longingly to a threatened future. Instead, we are preoccupied with the present. How am I going to get through today? How will I get by? What am I going to do? Who am I going to *be*? The questions associated with retirement are pressed all the more urgently by redundancy, and yet they are not the most painful demand. This is something with which we have been struggling for all these weeks and months during which we went on working. It is the demand to be told *when*.

Despite the fact that the overall economic situation in which the United Kingdom finds itself at the end of the twentieth century is responsible for the growing tide of redundancies, the shame at being 'laid off' still persists, particularly among those involved in commerce or the professions. This is not surprising. The various aspects of the 'retirement syndrome' which we have been looking at involve the kind of experience which is not wholly rational, or, at least, cannot be explained in terms of argued responses to the environment. Our need for power, for instance, is very far from being something which we are willing to acknowledge even if we are actually conscious of it. We know it is there because of what happens as a result of it; and the same is true of our various attitudes towards the social roles we play and their relationship to our unconscious life. We should not be surprised to find that the sense of wrongness which we feel when our jobs are taken away before the proper time comes across to us as some kind of personal shame, despite the fact that we know that it is happening to so many others and has nothing to do with our work record or our relationship with our bosses. The unconscious, more than the conscious, requires balance. Indeed, according to Jung, it is the origin of the urge towards wholeness and shape which we acknowledge in our conscious lives; time and the experience it brings with it carries us more into line with the unconscious pattern at the heart of our spiritual identity by which we conform to Identity itself, the final original, eternal Being who calls us home. Because we are time-bound, living from moment to moment, year to year, our need for pattern is expressed in the language of events, the way that the things that happen to us fall into line as part of a story, the story of our own life with its characteristic beginning, middle and end. In a very real sense the integrity of our identity depends on the recognizability of our life story. None of us knows how the story will end, but success at making some kind of personal sense of the past gives us confidence that the story will eventually reach some kind of satisfactory conclusion – or, at least, that it will make some kind of sense. We assume that the latter part of the story will be less eventful than the first, so that the points may be established, the arguments driven home, without departing from the main plot.

No doubt we should not be so sanguine about life challenges as to tell ourselves that we have learned to cope with them; we are certainly foolish to assume, as we always do, that we know *the kind of thing* that can happen and take appropriate action to mitigate its effects. The effects of being made redundant are never what one expects them to be because the event itself is so unexpected. The changes involved affect the way that we organize life at a deeper level than any contingency plans we may comfort ourselves that we have made. Even though, as we look about us at companies closing down, neighbours and friends 'on the scrap-heap', we feel frightened and anxious, the anxiety and fear we shall experience when it actually happens will be much more extreme and entirely different because when our story is shattered we are shattered also. I was almost there, we say to ourselves and other people. I could see the goalposts. I'm not interested in any other game.

The shock of severance may signal the onset of a typical grief reaction, which, one way or another, will follow its course through feelings of anger and self-reproach, and attempts to reproduce the situations and circumstances associated with the job that has been lost, until at last the world begins to show signs of renewed interest, and life begins again. Thus the emotional problems associated with some aspects of retirement are compounded by redundancy.

The result may not be entirely bad, however. In more than one case the shock of being made redundant has brought to the surface a powerful experience of loss, chaos and renewal that might have remained unacknowledged and unlived by the person concerned, and consequently have gone on troubling her or him much longer than it need have done. The trauma of redundancy is the burden of unfinished business, in which an unfinished task in the world is mirrored by a mind that goes on grieving. What I have just described is, after all, the classical grief reaction, the process of readjustment which, as we saw, accompanies every radical change in our experience of life. There is no doubt that it is, psychologically speaking, the only appropriate response to some of the life situations associated with retirement – at considerable cost to the individuals concerned in terms of personal anguish, that is. But there is more to it than this.

By restricting ourselves to individual responses to redundancy we are taking too narrow a view by far. Every redundancy rebounds psychologically upon the family and friends, as well as the former work-mates, business associates or professional colleagues, of the person concerned. What may seem to the employer to be the efficient rationalization of organizational procedures, disorganizes the organization of its community by substituting chaos for cosmos in individual families and social networks. The effect on local morale can be disastrous, so that to some extent this kind of action is always counter-productive, weakening the human base of the organization it aims at strengthening.

It is even worse when the aim is to destroy rather than to strengthen – when government policy demands the death of an industry and the dismissal of all concerned as no longer necessary: as redundant, in fact. We have recently seen an example of such widespread 'government action' when, in the autumn of 1992, thirty-one pits in the Yorkshire and Nottinghamshire coalfields were ordered to close down immediately. If the miners took strike action, they would lose their redundancy payments. Without going into the politics of this event – which took place without any kind of parliamentary or even Cabinet discussion, ('Just like it used ter be, on t'Gaffer's say so' – the Gaffer in this case being the Prime Minister) – it can be said that it resulted in protests from every direction, including MPs on the government side of the House of Commons. The Prime Minister's attempt to avoid total political disaster by postponing the closures and increasing severance pay did little to remove the sense of outrage. People spoke of 'the cynicism that seems to think you can buy people off with money'.

It was the effect of the blow upon the mining community, the individuals, families, villages and towns with their traditions of mutual support and their awareness of a common history binding them together, a shared identity rooted in a shared experience, that seized the imagination of the nation. Suddenly the miners became of the greatest value not only as individuals but as a group, a kind of people. Hardship had bound them together in the past, and they had learned how to look after one another in times of crisis, taking the pain of individuals into the heart of the caring community. From behind the barricades of region and class, the nation remembered these things now, and wept for the miners. 'The human cost', said Bishop Holloway of the Episcopal Church of Scotland, 'is totally unacceptable' – and the people of Britain agreed with him. Nobody was under any illusions about the government's intentions, even though execution had been temporarily stayed. Along with the miners themselves we were mourning the passing, not of a particular job, or a specific kind of society, but of an entire industry suddenly made redundant.

This, then, is the kind of thing that can happen nowadays. It calls for the toughest (in the sense of the most resilient and flexible) community care to look after its casualties. There is no reason to believe that any section of society is proof against the effect of the same 'market forces' that undermined the miners. An emotional reaction, an upsurge of feeling on behalf of the oppressed, is obviously not enough. Indeed, it can be worse than inadequate if it takes the place of action, as it often seems to do. To guard against the depersonalizing impact of being 'laid off' from the work on which you depend, in which your identity so largely abides, all kinds of humanizing influences and agencies are necessary. Indeed, there should ideally be a network of supportive systems, non-nuclear families all over the country, in every city, town, village and hamlet, ready to take the strain involved in agonizing social change, the birthpangs of the new society.

Perhaps it is time now to start investing the kind of energy and dedication in our church membership (for that is what I'm really talking about) that we do in our jobs and families. Church membership does not make the same kinds of demands as they do. In a sense it doesn't make any real demands at all, but is pure gift – although to allow the gift to be received as such involves a lot of hard work and dedication, as well as imagination and organizational experience. If you are capable of these things and are retired, then don't hold back! The Church needs you for the new form it will have to take in the future. Once again the Church is going to have to become its old-fashioned caring self, the self that showed how responsive it could be at times of social change, caring for the casualties of history, renewing the fibres of community by self-sacrificing actions and burdens lovingly borne.

It is impossible to overstress the importance of this. Once again the Christian Church is called to rediscover, and reassert, its ancient ministry of healing. What is involved here is much more than theology, much more than liturgy – although both theology and liturgy will draw from and contribute to it in terms of increased power to illuminate the lives of men and women. This renewal of Christian relevance concerns basic human solidarity. The kind of revision of Church priorities the situation calls for would directly affect the social fabric of the nation. It is impossible to be precise about the practical details of how such a thing would happen: each social group, each family and group of families would have to find its own way of proceeding, because every set of circumstances is bound to be different – outwardly similar, perhaps, but different at heart, and it is the heart that counts.

However, this does not stop me passing my own personal judgement on the situation and its needs. For this to happen, there must be a noticeable lessening of the Church's pre-occupation with human hierarchies, its own and other people's. There must be a genuine desire for equality within the social arrangements of the Body of Christ. Again, this primary aim is to be put into practice according to circumstances; but we should start at home, wherever our home happens to be. We should strive to increase people's sense of belonging together by our own ways of being and doing as Christians. Let the Church live the Gospel in a new way, one which is able to convince people that *it really knows* what it is like to be alive in the world as it is. Let the Church really take account of the world and not simply stand back and talk about it. There have been times in the past when Christians have been seen to care in such a way, times when the Church has been able to overcome the barriers of class, age, sex and occupation, the snobbery and opportunities for discrimination which characterize the normal ways of organizing itself.

The hallmark of Christian organization should be community rather than competition; perhaps the energy of those who have lost their jobs in this sudden, harsh and unexpected way could contribute to a new kind of Christian approach to the task of living together. People who have been victims of a ruthless social and political system will turn with relief to another way of relating people to people in community. They can only do this if the Church itself becomes more democratic, less rooted in historical differences and contemporary prejudices; but they can help it to do so, perhaps.

Fifteen years ago, Janet, Alan, Marian and Bill formed a church fellowship group of a new kind – one that was new then, anyway. They were all members of various congregrations: Janet an Anglican, Alan a Roman Catholic, Bill and Marian members of two Methodist churches that had split apart and gone their own ways round about the turn of the century. Apart from the fact that they were all churchgoers, the four had little in common: they came from different parts of the country; Janet was twenty-two, much younger than the other three, two of whom (Alan and Bill) were married, each with a family. Marian was unmarried, and cared for an aged mother. There was one thing they did have in common, however.

During the last few months each of them had been made redundant. Hearing of Alan's misfortune, Janet contacted him in order to offer what help she could. It was, she said, harder for people who were really established in their jobs – she had only been working for four years. It was Alan's idea that they should try to form some kind of network – not a club, said Janet, I can't stand clubs. She pointed out that it would be better to avoid any suggestion of exclusiveness: 'After all, we're the ones who've been excluded.' Alan brought Bill along (they were both from the same factory) and Janet recruited Marian.

These four formed the nucleus of the network. From the beginning there was a good deal on the agenda apart from mutual support. The group spent a long time wondering how it could organize itself to provide some kind of useful community service. 'We want something that will really express who we are and what we believe,' said Marian. 'Well, we know what we believe, don't we?' Alan said; and from that moment the idea of a specifically Christian objective for the group began to develop. Perhaps it is not surprising that, having been made redundant, they should look to their church roots. 'When you are suddenly cut off right in the middle of things, you find yourself reaching out for something more stable,' said Alan. 'The world you thought was so very firm, suddenly turns out to be very shaky. That's when you start thinking again,' Bill said.

For a time the network worked along more or less orthodox lines as a prayer and study group functioning for the benefit of its own membership, and drawing people from all four congregations. Most of its members continued to be recruited from among those who had been made redundant, although people lucky enough to get jobs still kept up their association ('a better word than "membership" ') with the network. As time went on, however, it became apparent that the distinctive thing about the network was, in fact, its inter-church identity. It was doing more to bring the various Christian Churches together than anything had ever done before, despite all the efforts that a better-than-average local Christian Council had put in over the years. It took several years, certainly, during which time the network continued to keep a low profile and work behind the scenes for greater Christian understanding and a more effective use of Church resources in the struggle to reflect the light of Christ in a selfish and rejecting world. Five years after the network began, an ecumenical service was held in the Roman Catholic church 'to celebrate the contribution to our Churches of men and women who have been made redundant'. By then, only Alan and Marian remained of the original four, but Janet and Bill, both of whom had managed to find work in other parts of the country, came over to the service. They were overjoyed to be able to come. 'It's wonderful', said Janet, 'to know that what united us as individuals has drawn us together as Churches.'

8. Ageing

This is not a book about ageing: that is, not specifically about the ageing process. There is no doubt, however, that the problems of retirement mentioned so far are compounded by the simple ordinary business of growing old. For some people this is a frightening idea, an area of life which they would rather not think about. They are preoccupied with the idea that, however old they may be, they will certainly get older; the limitations they are conscious of will get worse; the chance of illness will be greater, and they will be at the mercy of the kindness and the cruelty of younger people. Look how hard I worked, they will say, and look what has happened to me after all!

I have met few people over seventy-five who don't say this kind of thing from time to time, and a lot of folk say it when they are much younger than that! It seems to me to be very natural. It is too much to expect people to spend so much time seeking more money, influence, power, respect, admiration, opportunity for self-expression and ego-fulfilment without needing to dismiss from their awareness everything that is not immediately relevant, such as a state of affairs in which these things will have largely lost their appeal, at least in the forms they used to take. No doubt some goals will remain: less ambitious, more urgent, almost certainly defined in ways that are totally different from the older ones, so that those old ones seem, in turn, almost completely irrelevant.

On the other hand, thank God, there is the evidence of all those aged people who say that they are happier and more at peace with themselves now the struggle is largely over than they ever were 'in the front line'. If we are to believe C.G. Jung, this is because they have maintained contact with two psychological principles of integrative power. The archetypes of the Great Mother and the Wise Old Man operate at the deepest level of psychic awareness in order to calm our fear of change and to unite our individual consciousnesses with truth that is universal and divine: truth that brings wisdom in maturity and zest in old age. Whether or not one accepts Jung's ideas about archetypes and the 'collective unconscious', the fact remains that some people do achieve a remarkable serenity as they grow older, the condition that psychologists refer to as 'maturation', which, theoretically at least, continues until death. And they do it by refusing to run away from the image of age which is in their hearts. The prayer life of the church is immeasurably enriched by these people. It has been suggested that prayer networks might be set up in and between churches, so that those who are entering the time of life when physical mobility is limited may work creatively as intercessors within the family of the congregation, rather than in isolation, as is so often the case. Perhaps they could pray on our behalf for the things we find so difficult!

I am quite sure that the ability to contemplate our own old age is a faithful activity. If we believe that we are in God's hands, and that he loves us so much that he sent his son to share his own living and dying with us, then not only the years of our strength and potency but our whole life has meaning. Pain, or an extreme degree of discomfort, has the effect of distracting the mind from any possibility of peaceful thoughts; on the other hand, pain is frequently said by those suffering it to have a focusing effect. One need not expect that illness, if and when it comes, will totally destroy one's freedom to hope and to trust. My experience as a hospital chaplain has had the effect of reassuring me on this point. You do not have to be a saint, or even a particularly brave person, to 'die well'.

All the same, many people do fear death, which is why

101

they hesitate to mention it. Many more, I believe, fear it sometimes, usually when some significant event in their lives manages to batter a hole in, or creep round the side of, their defences. When somebody they love dies, certainly; or when they find themselves watching a television programme they meant to avoid; or when they are fortuitously reminded of some ancient, long-forgotten grief. There are many things that bring our mortality home to us: things that simply make us feel older, more dependent, less able to fend for ourselves. We begin to feel that other people, younger people, are colluding to hustle us off before our time – not so absurd a suggestion in the light of what sociologists are beginning to refer to as 'social death'. Michael Mulkay and John Ernst describe how 'From the time of retirement, elderly people in Britain and the US are channelled collectively away from the main areas of social activity and their social ties with the wider society are progressively weakened in anticipation of their biological end.' We should be fully aware that these restrictions on our personhood are not simply 'in the mind'. They are definitely there in society. But they present a challenge as well as a threat, one that retirees are beginning more and more to want to take up: witness the immense popularity of the TV series *Waiting for God*. Unlike its biological analogue, social death is something that may be resisted!

How to learn to do it, at this age? How to adjust to a new, reduced (as we may see it) role when flexibility seems to be a thing of the past? The answer is, of course, that it isn't. People can adjust to new situations all their lives. Obviously, if you have been doing the same kind of thing in the same kind of social setting for twenty or thirty years, your ability to change will be a bit rusty. Rusty or not, it will still be there, and when you have succeeded in adapting to the new situation you will be extremely pleased with yourself, particularly when people congratulate you on having 'settled down so well'. (You may even come to be pleased when they add 'at your age'!)

The fact is, of course, that ageing presents its own solutions as well as its problems. Because we are getting older, we tend to confuse the two categories: because *we* are getting older we find it difficult to stand back for a clear look. It is happening to *us*: we are not in the best position to say what will turn out well and what not so well. Perhaps, at the moment, we don't want to change at all, even for the better! We would rather cling to what we've got, what we know. Conversations with old people, both men and women, some of them suffering from illness or handicap, lead me to believe that this state of mind is temporary.

People at retirement age, whether they are women of sixty or men of sixty-five, do not welcome change because it reminds them of the final change. There is every reason to believe, however, that this particular anxiety, in its acute form, belongs to the present rather than the future, and that it will become less intense once retirement is accepted as a way of life. On the other hand, if the idea of dying is not so aversive that it has perpetually to be denied, the prospect of this antecedent 'life change' will not cause so much discomfort. Certainly, it is in the tradition of Christian spirituality to regard every major landmark in life as a rehearsal for dying, death itself being the final transformation scene. None of these changes (and we must include retirement among them) is achieved without pain. We have seen how every existential transformation involves a period of emotional and intellectual turmoil which intervenes between the old and the new without being able to draw strength from either. Overlooking these periods of 'pivotal chaos', we tend to look back on life as something that has progressed smoothly, experience giving way to experience without the pitfalls that occur whenever we have to endure genuine change.

The kinds of difficulties I described when I was talking about change may be harder to come to terms with when we are older than they were earlier because we are more set in our ways; but we have learned something about the problem of adjusting to change by now, and are not so surprised by the things it throws up in our faces; horrified perhaps, disturbed, certainly discouraged, but no longer surprised. Age does, after all, bring experience. It allows us to take the longer view, look to the broader horizon. To a certain extent it helps us avoid making the same mistakes twice. The traumatic effect of change subsists largely in the unexpectedness of the trauma; because we expected things to go smoothly we are at a loss to find ourselves suddenly so upset. We don't know why we feel like this, nor how long it will last. Later on in life we still have the same kind of experience; but now we know more about it. Firstly, we know that it belongs to change itself, rather than to our own ability to cope with change. Secondly, we know that it will not last for ever. Thirdly, we are no longer surprised that it hurts, although we may have forgotten how much.

All the same, there is no getting round the fact that age brings severe practical disadvantages, which almost inevitably outweigh any increase in stoicism we may be capable of. As the years pass we are more likely to become ill, either temporarily or permanently, to a greater or lesser extent; our mobility grows more restricted, the range of activities within our reach more circumscribed. When all this happens we are better off without the pressures and pains of having to hold down a full-time job. We press on towards retirement age with grim determination; we couldn't really go on working any longer because we really feel we are 'past it'. Because they can currently retire five years before men, it might be expected that women would be less likely to reach this desperate condition; but such conditions do not really amount to much, as illness and accident are no respecters of age and sex, and married women are invariably within our society expected to go on doing at least half their customary work even when retired – unless, of course, they can persuade their spouses to share the housework with them. This is why, despite their 'extra' years, they do not really have more time in which to practise being retired. Only those who

104

take early retirement can do this, and they may very well prefer to have been able to go on working.

When I have spoken about dying up to now it has usually been in some kind of symbolic connection – for instance, when we looked at our normal fear and dislike of life changes I suggested that the idea of change disturbs us because it reminds us of where, biologically speaking, change eventually leads. I suggested, too, that changes which involve a loss of control over people and things in our everyday environment tend to suggest a state of being in which we have no power at all, simply because we are no longer alive. The fear of death can have a much more immediate cause than this, however. It can be brought to mind by the actual evidence of mortality which we carry with us every day of our lives, however happy and well we may be at any given moment. As human beings we are aware of being intensely vulnerable; notice how quickly we step aside if we think somebody might be going to step on our foot. This immediate state of proneness to disaster is the real presence of death in our lives.

Apart from the fear of dying there is the business of living, and this inevitably gets harder as we become older. Thus, as our consciousness of the need to take our mind off the subject grows, so it becomes harder and harder to turn a blind eye to the things that have begun to go wrong with our ability to function the way we used to when we were younger. This is the point at which, with many of us, the fear of dying gives place to the more pressing business of simply keeping alive. We would be advised to admit the fact that we are getting old, that our bodies and minds are no longer capable of doing all the things they used to do, and that we are going to need help; if we don't already, that is.

Some people realize this before they reach retirement age and retire early on grounds of invalidity. This means that they are able to draw 'invalidity benefit' from the state, and to go on doing so even when they have reached the normal retirement age and are receiving the Old Age Pension. There is a drawback, however: if you are receiv-

ing an invalidity allowance there is a limit imposed on the
amount you can earn by doing any kind of job. You may
feel perfectly well most of the time, and would welcome
the chance to be gainfully employed once again. Nevertheless, you are officially too ill to do a proper job and must
content yourself with just pottering. The trouble is, you
don't feel properly retired; you just weren't old enough.
The other side of this coin concerns those who felt perfectly well until they retired, and now suddenly feel old
and useless. Like the others, they eventually accept the
inevitable, although they may need a good deal of understanding and support on the way. There is only one inevi-
tability; the problem is that different people have different
ways of coming to terms with it, and nobody is in control
of all the circumstances in which they must do this. The
worst thing we can do in this connection is to expect
others to adjust to death, their own or someone else's, in
the ways *we* think are appropriate.

There are signs of an increasing interest in, and respect
for, old age. The battered stereotype of knitting needles
and walrus moustaches is not quite so popular as it was,
nor so universally accepted as accurate. Someone has
started a network of study groups run for pensioners by
pensioners, called 'The University of the Third Age'. This
has branches in many parts of the United Kingdom. So
many retired people are enrolled in courses at universities
and colleges that the student of seventy-five who has just
received her PhD hardly attracts any publicity, except for
a brief TV newsflash. As the number of elderly people
increases so the proportion of them taking an active part
in community affairs grows, and with this the image of
an elderly person as someone with the resources of experience and the wisdom of maturity gains a firmer hold on
the national consciousness.

Seven couples and one widower live in Hurst Avenue, all
of them of retirement age, which is why it is kown locally
as 'Retirement Row'. Hugh is the only person living there
by himself. He is still acutely conscious of this, although

it is five years since his wife died. He is sixty-three and Helen was fifty-five when the fatal accident occurred. People keep telling Hugh that 'It's early days'; they have been saying this for five years. Hugh has several friends in 'The Row'. In fact, he's on good terms with all the couples who live there. In a way this makes things worse, bringing home Helen's absence to an almost intolerable degree. Hugh has decided that he will see as little as possible of them, simply because the presence of people who knew Helen is very painful, while people who knew them both are to be avoided at all costs. So he keeps out of the way.

The other residents of 'The Row' are hurt by this behaviour, although they understand the reason for it. They can remember a time when Hugh used to talk about taking early retirement so that he could enjoy 'doing the garden and chatting like the rest of you'. That was before Helen was killed in the road accident and life stood still. Now the only thing was to keep on working. Teaching was something he did almost without thinking, certainly without worrying how to do it. He was respected rather than loved at school, because of his rather withdrawn and preoccupied manner. After his wife's death, however, people began to see a change in him: he was friendlier and more approachable than he used to be, more willing to ask about your family and show more interest in what you were doing. After all those years of being on the outside, Hugh found himself growing quite popular.

Perhaps this had something to do with his being willing to invest more of himself in his job nowadays. It seemed to him that his school was his real home, the only one he had now. He would leave the house as soon as he could and arrive at school before anyone else, having snatched a bacon and egg sandwich at a café on the way over. He would hang on as long as he could when everyone else had gone home, to the annoyance of the school caretaker, who wondered what the heck had happened to the old man. Hugh was not all that old, actually, only just sixty, although he looked considerably older. Those who knew

107

him said that he had put on ten years at least since Helen died. It wasn't surprising, they said. He'd suffered a terrible blow.

For Hugh, school had become a substitute home. He spent as much time there during the day as he could, and had every intention of putting off retirement as long as possible. 'Before it happened I was all set to take early retirement, so that we could get about a bit and enjoy ourselves. We thought we deserved it. I know Helen did.' This was the paradise that they had promised each other, and the symbolic measure of his loss. Now he could hardly bear to open the front door when he got home. Sometimes, on particularly bad days, he didn't go home at all. He would get as far as the front gate then walk round the corner to ring up his daughter and ask if he might stay the night at her house. Meanwhile, he threw himself into his job, fully intending to go on as long as he possibly could. He didn't know that the ache in his knees was the beginning of arthritis, which was to develop rapidly and force him to retire at sixty-two. Now he is more or less housebound, although he does manage to get out to sit in the garden. He likes to do this when the neighbours are gardening, so that he can talk over the fence to them. He has been offered a place in an old people's home, and could afford to go private if he wanted. However, he prefers to stay in his own home as long as he can, 'near my friends'.

Hugh is still not sure whether he ever retired. Life, somehow, got in the way. Life, and the business of growing old. If you have continued reading this far you will probably have gathered by now that I am myself round about retirement age. In fact, very many church people are, as the French say, 'd'un certain age'. The pastoral ministry is largely concerned with women and men in the second half of life, with all the problems that this brings with it; for example, the appalled recognition that we can remember things that happened fifty or sixty years ago better than what the Church Treasurer said at the last PCC meeting; the temptation to fight and re-fight battles lost many years ago; the growing dread of becoming restricted in one's freedom and dependent upon others; the fear about *how* we shall die, which perhaps never completely vanishes, even when we think we are ready to depart. These and many more are the matters concerning retirement that strike home to priests and ministers. These are the things we should be addressing. If we were not so taken up with the perpetual desire to capture the attention of youth we should have time to turn our attention to those who are actually asking for our help. The briefest, most cursory glance at the Old and New Testaments is enough to remind us of the importance of the part played by the elderly in the history of salvation from Noah to John the Evangelist, taking in Abraham and Sara, Moses, Zacharias and Elisabeth, Simeon and Anna, all of them lights to their own generations, some of them considerably more than that. And yet, how often do we hear a sermon about the Bible's attitude to age? Surely there is something that could be done about this!

It would take more than the occasional sermon, of course, although that might be a beginning, enough to attract the attention of this much-neglected section of the congregation so that it might become more vocal. Once the consciousness of the congregation has been heightened to the pitch at which some kind of activity is called for, it should be possible to create ways of including programmes of study and discussion within the continuing life of the congregation. A study group on 'The Christian Doctrine of Age', for instance, would be based on Biblical material but could be extended to take in other literature. What about discussions about the relationship between generations within the congregation and in society as a whole? The actual reminiscences of elderly worshippers are an endless source of fascination, with the insights that they so often give rise to about what church life really felt like many years ago. These things should not be merely passed over as if they had no relevance for us and for our problems of relating to one another and organizing our churches; they represent the testimony of experience, the

109

terms on which our current reality exists, and so the underlying structure of any futures we find ourselves planning. The young businessman who is so certain about the way the parish should go forward would do well to note the faint smile on the lips of his fellow PCC member who has been 'going to St Luke's since the church was first built'. When Tom says he's seen it all, it may be annoying. It may also be true. And Tom also saw what happened next.

9. Opportunity

Peter's children were extremely proud of their father, although they didn't see him very often, at least not while they were small. When they did, when for a few precious weeks each year he was at home, going about with them like other people's fathers, trying to atone for months of ordinary absence with a few short days of extra-ordinary presence, then they simply made the best of things. After all, it wasn't every family that had a ship's captain for its father. When he was at home it was marvellous; they all had a wonderful time; then he went back to sea until he came home again. You always knew where he was when your friends asked about him. The first thing you learned when you were little was where Daddy was. All the family carried maps of the world's trade routes. It gave you a sense of identity, made you feel rather special.

When he reached the age of fifty, Peter left the sea and took a shore job. His eldest daughter and son were married by now, and the two younger daughters were both students at the local polytechnic. Peter never really felt that he behaved like an ordinary father to them, having missed so much of the essential early training for it: 'By the time I came on the scene in anything like a permanent kind of way they were all grown up. They seemed to know so much more about life than I did. I get on all right with them, thank goodness; but I always feel more like a friend than a father.' When he says this, people point out how extremely lucky he is, considering some of the things that seem to get in the way of ordinary families, where the parents would give a good deal to be able to say they were on anything like friendly terms with their children. Peter knows this well enough, of course. He hastens to point out that he isn't ungrateful. In the meantime, however, he is waiting for the children to get married and have children of their own. This time he will make quite sure that he isn't away on his own business while there are people growing up around him. Peter and his wife had to wait several more years before grandchildren arrived. The babies, a boy and a girl, lived a hundred miles away from their grandparents, which meant that Peter could only see them rarely, so long as he was still working. Even when the children's parents were able to bring them over to see their grandparents, Peter couldn't always depend on getting time off. The coming of more babies simply intensified the problem, adding to the frustration of having to go on working away, separated by hundreds of miles from his developing family. Roll on retirement, and the opportunity to rediscover one's lost parenthood.

There are thousands of people like Peter, of course. Men and women who can't wait to retire in order to enjoy the extra opportunities of one kind or another that freedom from full-time working will bring. They have to be careful, or they will end up working harder than ever, particularly if they have useful hobbies – useful to other people, that is! All the same, most people find there is a very real difference between working because you're paid to do it, and labouring away at things you yourself have chosen to do, even though they don't provide a wage packet. The secret is freedom, the urge to make your own decisions and plan your own life. With a lot of us, this urge is in abeyance for many years, while we concentrate on the urgent business of making a living or bringing up a family (or both). It's surprising how it awakens to life when the prospect of retirement draws near!

For Peter, freedom simply means the chance to see his grandchildren more often. We can only hope that he shows some restraint, and doesn't get in the way too much. At least he knows he will be useful in his new role, and that his children will be able to get out and enjoy some social life for a change. No doubt Peter will find plenty to do during his retirement. At the moment, however, he's not thinking about things to do, but *people to be with*. And why not?

Up to now I have painted a rather gloomy picture of retirement. I was determined that the difficulties and challenges lying just beneath the surface of this very ordinary event in people's lives should not be passed over. In the case of some unlucky people these things – surrender of authority, confusion about identity and role, inability to lay the past to rest, guilt at not having to work so hard and so *faithfully* – really do present major problems, lying in wait like icebergs beneath the surface of the calm, even course they have plotted for their life in retirement. It's a good idea to know about these things, even if you think that they will never apply to you. They are perfectly normal factors in our reaction to important changes in the way we organize our lives, so we should be aware of them 'just in case'. Apart from this we ought to take note of what might affect other people, even if we ourselves manage to steer a safe course into calmer waters.

Having said this, I turn (with some relief, I admit) to what I have neglected up to now, except for a few brief mentions here and there. This is the 'other side' of retirement: retirement as opportunity and hope, the time of life when long-cherished dreams are realized, new horizons are discovered, neglected aspects of the personality are developed; the time when people are able at last to concentrate their energies on being themselves and appreciating one another; the time when schedules are forgotten, clocks can be ignored, and you can give yourself permission to relax at last. This is all true, in the sense that these things are all real facts of our psychological life, just as the other, more depressing things were. We may not be able to achieve all of them, but we have a very good chance of getting nearer than we are now to some of them. Retirement is the time of *opportunity*, when plans that have been cherished for many years can sometimes be brought to

113

fulfilment. Some people do amazing things with their new freedom, embarking on adventures which are complete reversals of the way in which they have previously organized their lives. For example, an ex-member of Her Majesty's Secret Service retired to Cornwall in order to live on a cliff and write books popular with cat lovers; a Welsh schoolteacher took early retirement in order to go to RADA and thence to the Royal Shakespeare Company; a successful journalist, well-known for her ability to excoriate the male sex, retired to Surbiton and married a boy she went to school with.

These are just three cases chosen at random. A visit to the Scottish Highlands, or West Cornwall, or any number of other places, will lead to the discovery of hundreds of retired people, emigrants from other parts of the country now running small businesses or tea shops and 'country crafts', wresting a well-deserved pension supplement from the earth or the sea. Even retirement to the South Coast, although not quite so adventurous, does not have to be so dull as it sounds. The imagination, after all, acknowledges no boundaries, and some of the greatest first books ever written have emerged from places very like Bournemouth. Poetry, said Wordsworth, is 'emotion recollected in tranquillity'. This does not need to be Langdale Fell. It could just as easily happen in the course of a short walk between the pier and the Jubilee Gardens. Anyone who has ever written a book will tell you this.

In the same way, just as some people spend years putting off writing 'their' book, so others look forward to getting down to some really serious studying. It may be something they started earlier in life and are waiting for a chance to get back to, or it may be a completely new subject: 'One day I'll get a chance to get down to finding out about those rocks over there. They've been staring me in the face for the last thirty years!' You don't need to go to university to do this, although you may be able to do so if you're suitably qualified (and motivated!). Various colleges have 'distance learning' (home study) courses, and university extramural departments make a range of subjects easily accessible. The courses run locally by the Workers' Educational Association (WEA) provide excellent introductions to various subjects, leading onwards to the possibility of more advanced study. Most exciting of all is the University of the Third Age, set up some years ago and already spreading out over the country. This is a self-help group of retired people whose aim is the sharing of knowledge and experience gained over many years for the stimulation of the mature understanding. A really creative way of learning and teaching at the same time.

This is a subject close to my own heart. Because I left school early I never had the opportunity to go to university, and this has always been a matter of regret. My father, with the help of *The Times Literary Supplement* and Mudie's Library, had read almost everything, or seemed to have done, and my childhood ambition was to equal his erudition, or even perhaps surpass it. It was not to be, however. Circumstances, including illness, going into the army, getting married, led me in other directions. I went to drama school and, later on, to theological college, but never to university. I later spent eighteen years as a full-time chaplain in a psychiatric hospital, studying on the side, taking courses at local universities as a part-time student. It was all very interesting but, of course, it had to take second place to my *real* work: first of all as an actor, then as a priest. Now I am retired and can turn all my attention to what I really wanted to do in the first place. Studying, I believe, is my vocation. There is a character in Chekhov's play *The Seagull* who describes his profession as that of 'perpetual student'. His name is Trigorin and he plays a crucial role in the plot. I identify with him completely. I don't know why I'm so keen on studying. I like to write, certainly, and the concentration helps keep my mind going (or so I tell myself). There's just something about being a student. It seems to keep me young. Other people tell me that it all concerns my relationship with my father: I'm trying to impress him still, forty years on. Perhaps I am – but that doesn't seem to me to be a good reason to deny myself the pleasure that I get from reading books and going to lectures. It seems a harmless kind of pursuit, after all. And now I can throw myself into it in a way that I never could before. The result of this is that it has assumed a new significance in my life. Because, at last, I have been able to bring my feelings about it into the forefront of my awareness, I have started to organize my personality with regard to it, to take it properly into account in the way that I regard myself. It has always been there, you see. However, because it was always there it exerted a distracting influence when my official business lay elsewhere. Now I can bring it into focus and keep it there. At last it can play the part in my life that it deserves.

Of course, this sort of thing doesn't suit everybody. We haven't all got unfulfilled ambitions and unrealized dreams that we are longing to fulfil or realize. Not everybody wants to do something completely different when they retire. People who enjoy their job may want to find some way of maintaining a connection with it, either on a voluntary basis, or as a hobby, or simply by keeping in touch with people still doing it. Some people (clergymen, for instance) never really retire at all, because their services are always needed and they are paid for what they do in retirement. (There is an obvious danger here; clergy who are officially retired seem inclined to shorten their own lives by working even harder than they did before! Perhaps lay people can do something to help make them see sense.) Other people (lawyers, for instance) are relieved that they no longer bear the responsibility for how things are done, but can still help out as advisers or consultants. Others simply enjoy being around, like the retired railwayman leaning on the fence at the bottom of the garden, shouting advice to the shunters.

Most people, I think, don't want much to change, except for not having to get up for work. They want to relax, wait a bit and see what happens. They might think about doing something later on – take a part-time job, for instance – but not yet. And not if it involves too much hassle, either. They are certainly not looking for a substitute for the job they are leaving behind. What, they say, is the point of that? I've worked hard for a long time. Now I want to enjoy my rest. At last I'm free to do what I choose: and I choose to do nothing. Can you blame me?

The trouble is that people don't seem to know how to rest. This is not surprising, seeing that they have worked all their lives. For thirty, forty, almost fifty years they have trained to be non-relaxers. The question is, how shall we help them learn to *do* very much less, so that they may come to *be* a lot more? It's a matter of time: not only the time we can spare for the job, but the way we and the person we are trying to help regard time itself. This may seem an odd thing to say, but I believe it lies right at the heart of the fear that afflicts so many people when they are faced with the prospect of finally stopping working. Even the phrase sounds ominous, as if our very ability to function as human beings depended on our keeping on labouring away, so that when the fatal day arrived, we simply 'stopped working'.

Only when we have learned to handle time better will we be able to contemplate this kind of change in our life with any kind of equanimity. So long as we are obsessed with the demands imposed upon us by the unforgiving minute, each one of us seeing life as an endless round of purposeful activity, an interlocking succession of tasks to be completed and challenges to be met, then every problem unsolved, or question to which we do not know the answer, presents us with a threat to our entire way of being. If our only purpose is to handle each situation that comes up, what shall we do when something happens that we have no idea how to deal with? It has taken us thirty years to learn the rules of this game. What shall we do when the referee blows his whistle on the only life we know, and the rules are changed?

In the working life of so many people time is a precious commodity; there never seems enough of it, we hoard it as if we thought it might suddenly run out on us. In fact, we are quite wrong about this. Time, *as we experience it*, is something qualitative rather than quantitative. We know

117

very well how subjective our impression is of the speed
at which things happen, how days can pass like lightning,
minutes drag like hours. We tend to think of this as an
indication of the degree to which we are enjoying ourselves, and it certainly does have to do with our state of
mind. We can be more precise about it than that, however.
When we are engaged in doing something that takes all
our attention, whether it is officially classed as 'work' or
as 'play', we feel we have experienced more in a shorter
time than our watches say has actually passed; if, on the
other hand, we aren't able to concentrate and thrash about
looking for something interesting, every minute is five
minutes long. The answer seems to lie in the degree of
engagement. If we can get 'stuck into' something time is
no longer an enemy, because when it runs out we are
ready to take a break anyway. As an indication of time's
real significance this is actually more realistic than literal
clock-watching. It is the way that we co-operate with time
instead of allowing it to rule us: more work actually gets
done, or more pleasure is enjoyed, in less measurable
time! What a pity life can't always be like this!

In fact, there is no valid reason why it shouldn't be. No
logical, scientific reason, that is. Physicists believe less and
less in 'absolute' time, valid for all situations. Theodor
Bovet, the Swiss psychiatrist, puts it like this:

> Time is not a hollow space existing in a vacuum in which we
> store our effects in the most appropriate way that is possible;
> we cannot arbitrarily dispose of time as we do with a sum of
> money or a commodity; on the contrary, we need to discover
> its particular structure for ourselves, and thereafter aim at that,
> just as a rabbit has environment and capacities different from
> those of an elephant or a swallow, and thus it must adjust
> accordingly.

Elsewhere, he says that 'time is the personal structure of
each existing life'.

It is generally assumed that people who are retired have
more of what we might call 'objective' time, or at least
that they have the opportunity to have more of it. They

will also probably have more opportunity to spend time doing what they like doing, or consider worth doing, instead of being bound by other people's judgement on the matter. This being so, they stand to benefit from the 'rate of temporal exchange': more work, or more play, in less time. At the same time, this is a privilege which has to be treated with respect, and not exploited. This is time to be worked *with*, not *against*. The time which deepens as our interest grows is a gift rather than a commodity. Perhaps we understand this better as we grow older, and cherish what we have left as a place to live in, a setting for enjoyment and fulfilment rather than a tool for subduing opposition – I can get there faster, I can do it quicker. Now our hope is that, hand in hand with time, we may find the peace of mind that comes from a better relationship with life, one that surpasses understanding: that is, reaches deeper and higher than the attempt to assert intellectual control over whatever may happen.

One of the aspects of 'real' time, time as the sphere of personal relationships, that concerns retired people most is the business of the readjustment of roles. This has been mentioned before in its wider application. Its relevance here is that our experience of time depends largely on our role relationships with other people. We are all affected by the division of labour within the community, no matter how small it may be, in which we live; when changes come which affect the life of that community, role relationships shift and change. Questions arise as to how the new situation will affect ordinary daily living; whether it will be necessary for individuals to change their routines by taking on new responsibilities and shedding old ones; whether it will be possible to find a new balance which will satisfy everybody and make the best of any new responsibilities that may arise; whether it would be better to carry on much as usual, only without the strain imposed by the working situation. Such questions need to be answered, carefully and with consideration for the feelings of everyone involved. Retirement is a time when couples can renegotiate their relationships. It gives partners the

119

opportunity, and the space outside routine pressures, to think again about how they would really like to arrange their lives: 'The children are grown up, the mortgage is paid off, you won't be expected at work in the morning. I've been thinking, you know. It occurred to me a long time ago that – if you think it's a good idea – '

And so it happens that husbands take up pottery and wives go into business to market the wares; wives drive mini-cabs and husbands learn dress-designing; couples whose professional lives never touched open seaside boarding houses, she acting as landlady, he as cook. The identity crises of retirement are resolved in a great variety of ways, all equally creative. Of course, it is possible to overlook this opportunity to rethink what your relationship is really about, and what you as a couple really want from life. If you do, it is highly unlikely that you will get another chance. The danger is that if you go on as if nothing at all had happened you will find yourself less free, and less happy, than ever before; retirement has a way of magnifying the weaknesses of a marriage without increasing its strengths. Suffice it to say that the way things worked out when one or both of you were working depended on the preservation of a finely adjusted balance of 'give and take'. That balance has been broken. A new one must somehow be found or you will both suffer – one, unfortunately, almost certainly more than the other. The question is, who is to do what? This takes precedence over any decision as to whether or not a retired person should find a way of going on working. This concerns the relationship of couples in the home: if it's wrong, or could be improved, now is the time to redesign it, to try and put it right: only when it's right can you safely look outside for an answer to boredom which will suit you both.

One reason why Joan was looking forward to Andrew's retirement was that it would give her a chance to drive the car again. If she could do this she would be able to branch out more with her hobby and part-time business, which was looking after unwanted cats. Andrew was a salesman, and spent a good deal of his time away from home; it would be marvellous to have him around more often. His arthritis wasn't getting any better, so he admitted that he was relieved not to have to drive so much any more, which meant that the car would be available for Joan's use. Joan waited for Andrew to suggest something along these lines, but he did not. So far as he was concerned *he* was the car driver, and that was that. Now that he didn't drive it, he didn't really see the point of keeping it on: 'It's quite an expense, you know.'

He was enjoying spending more time at home with Joan. It was no longer a case of 'passing like ships in the night'. For her part, Joan began to feel more and more hampered by his presence. Not having the car took away — her final chance of having some say in what they would do together. With some kind of transport perhaps something could be done about her own business without having to refer even routine decisions to him, which made her feel very dependent. Actually, Andrew had quite forgotten that she *could* drive. Funny the way, whenever she was about to tackle him about it, his arthritis began to play up.

Petra is five years older than her sister Alice. Consequently she retired from her Civil Service job five years earlier. Very much the older sister she has always been the head of the household, so that Alice sometimes felt that she thought her own (Alice's, that is) very important and onerous job was really just a way of keeping her out of trouble, and not to be compared with Petra's own career. Petra was getting older now, and more things were having to be shared, so far as the actual running of the house was concerned. The trouble was that Petra always had to be in charge of everything. Unless she was willing to allow Alice more equality, Alice's own imminent retirement would be simply a case of rather more of the same kind of thing.

In both these instances there are personality factors present which are unlikely to change in a radical way. Andrew and Petra are going to go on being rather selfish people, Joan will always be shy, and Alice will continue to have a tendency to nurse her anger instead of express-ing it. There are, however, things in the situation that could be changed so that the balance was better, the clash of personalities not so great.

I have found that a good deal can be done 'from the outside', so to speak. Retirement is a time when people do actually talk to other people about the changes which are happening in their lives. It seems that this is an accept-able thing to do, the implication being that 'people will understand', retirement being something that happens to so many people. By doing this, they let themselves in for all sorts of comments from acquaintances and friends, some of which are clichés confirming them in their own automatic reactions to what is happening to them, some of which are not. The fact is, it is sometimes easier for someone who is not a close family member to say what needs to be said than it is for somebody caught up in the actual situation, bound hand and foot by things that have happened, feelings that have been expressed, attempts at communication that have failed in the past. I am sure that the pastoral care of newly retired people involves a certain amount of willingness to intervene in this way, to seize the opportunity afforded by times in people's lives when events arrive at a turning point, and personal relationships become more intense, and therefore, to a certain extent, more public. At these times the structure of a relationship is more readily discernible to those not closely involved. A gentle question about the car from someone who knew both Andrew and Joan turned out to be all that was needed to release the vehicle and readjust the situation. Petra's and Alice's case required more persistence, and involved a good deal of purposeful conversation about Alice's job, initiated by a concerned friend of both sisters. This was for the purpose of educating Petra about aspects of her little sister's life of which she was unaware. Whether or not it had this effect is open to question. On the other hand it certainly encouraged Alice a good deal, and helped her to speak up for herself more.

The point is, these interventions took place at a time

when the social significance of personal events became more clearly visible. When we reach an important turning point in our life, things that we and other people take for granted as being our own business, private and confidential, 'just between us', rise to the surface for ourselves and other people. It may actually be that other people see them first, as we prefer to talk about something else. We do want to talk, particularly when the principal subject confers some degree of credit on us: as, for instance, when we are retiring from a position which we have held for thirty years and have a beautiful gold watch to show for it. Behind the major theme there is a lot of other information that could probably do with being communicated and stands a better chance of seeing the light now than at most other times. Kelly describes how the creative process always involves letting go of the firm mental grip we have of the stock of interlocking ideas and their associated emotional reactions that has served us so well, and allowing new patterns to emerge, which in turn become established as we use them for living. Just as creativity necessitates a time of 'loosening' followed by one of 'tightening', so the shake-up of the kaleidoscope of our family arrangements which takes place at retirement allows new patterns to emerge. This is particularly significant with regard to the fixed ideas that we have about male and female roles, both in society and the family. Retirement is a particularly important time in our lives, specifically because it presents us with an opportunity to renegotiate our male–female relationships with the people closest to us. Once freed from the sexual stereotyping that restricts our activities throughout our working lives, we can discover ways of thinking, feeling and behaving, that we have not even bothered to consider, simply because we regard them as the exclusive property of the other sex, to be experimented with only at the very greatest risk to one's own personal identity. Male and female were like two adjoining countries; cross the frontier and you might never get back *home* again! Almost exclusive concentration on the sexual differences involved in procreation, and the

123

social (and consequently personal) problems associated with any kind of blurring of the division between the sexes in this particular area of life, has resulted in our refusal to explore the psychic territory that both sexes share together. Instead, ideas, attitudes, tendencies, feelings which belong to both sexes are rigidly divided up and apportioned between them.

C.G. Jung has one answer. There are, he says, some things about people that are specifically either male or female, apart from their obvious sexual identity. But to ascribe the female characteristics to women, and the male to men, is to miss the point entirely. In our unconscious life, which is always affecting our conscious awareness, we are both female and male, both male and female. We experience our contra-sexual components through our relationship with someone of the other sex; according to Jung we actually choose somebody who represents our own inner psychic identity. Creative men 'give birth' to the things they produce through their own inner femininity, and the unconscious male in a woman brings forth the seeds of creativity which are able to fertilize her own femininity. Animus and anima, the male and female psychic principles, dominate Jungian psychology, the first associated with 'spirit', the second with 'soul'. He himself was quite definite about the vital role they play in human awareness:

> The anima is an archetypal form, expressing the fact that a man has a minority of female genes . . . it is constantly present, and it works as a female in a man . . . it is the same with the animus. It is a masculine image in a woman's mind which is sometimes quite conscious, sometimes not conscious.

This was taken from an informal conversation. Jung added that the animus is called into life the moment a woman meets a man who says the right things. Then, because he says it, it is all true, no matter what he is. This is also so with the man concerned, of course. It is the reason why the sexes are able to identify not only each other, but also *with* each other. It depends, of course, on our being sufficiently in touch with our own psychic life that we 'resonate' to the other person, whose image we carry within us. As we have already suggested, life crises, because they involve the disturbance of set patterns, and the onset of times of confusion and instability, may provide an opportunity for devising new ways of arranging life, which need not necessarily be inferior to the old ones.

It would be a pity if they were, because this would definitely mean that an opportunity had been missed which might not come again; at least, not in the same way. The time of life when most people retire (that is, some time between fifty-five and seventy) is a very important one from the point of view of their psychological development. Jung tells us that these are the years during which we become conscious of our true identity. Other psychologists appear to concentrate mainly on the psychic life of young people, but with Jung it is different. He views the passing years in a much more optimistic way, seeing advancing age as the opportunity for increasing peace of mind. For one thing, it should be possible to be in dialogue with one's contra-sexual self, instead of having to defend oneself from any awareness of his or her existence, and from the fact that he or she 'has a different viewpoint from my conscious one'.

For Jung, listening to one's unconscious mind is a very important activity, because it is in doing so that one learns precious things about oneself. These are things that truly belong to one's soul's health. They do not simply represent material which has been repressed for defensive purposes, and now must be recognized and then summarily dealt with by being included within the understanding, filed away in the drawer marked consciousness. Jung's attitude towards the unconscious is very different from Freud's. He sees it as an Aladdin's cave of hidden riches, the richness of the true self, so long ignored and overlooked by so many people.

The richness, however, emerges in the dialogue, or 'dialectical discussion', as conscious and unconscious animus and anima (or anima and animus in the case of a woman)

125

give life and expression to one another. 'To be whole means to become reconciled with those sides of the personality which have not been taken into account, because they have been largely unconscious,' says Freda Fordham in her classic book about Jung. Jung himself strikingly describes the result: 'It is as if a river that had run to waste in sluggish side-streams and marshes, suddenly found its way back to its proper bed.' The name given to this gradual flowering of the self is 'individuation' – the quest for wholeness, necessitating forging a link between conscious and unconscious aspects of the psyche – 'an experience', Fordham comments, 'which can also be formulated as the finding of God within'. She goes on to say that it is this process involving the reconciliation of the opposing trends in our natures which develops gradually within a person's life, and more noticeably in the second half of life.

Ideas like these have been of very great help to me in my own pastoral work. However, I realize that they by no means represent mainstream Christian theology, and that some Christians may regard them with suspicion, despite Jung's own profound religious convictions, and his stated belief in God's son as our redeemer. This is not the point, however. What I mean to say in this chapter is that retirement, like other life crises, is a point of growth. Like other life crises, it has an effect of opening life out, disclosing its strengths and weaknesses. There is no doubt at all that things come to the surface at these times which must be taken seriously, and not simply ignored. Some of these things present an opportunity for change, change in the direction of growth, which frequently means some kind of reconciliation between ideas, demands, feelings that have coexisted almost entirely at the expense of one another. The protective carapace of normal life, daily routine, social convention, has hidden these factors in the situation from view. Once they have been uncovered and duly recognized there is a possibility that they may somehow be brought into relationship with one another. And then, *real* change may occur.

With regard to voluntary work, though, a word of warning. This kind of work is 'self-sanctioned' – basically, you decide whether you want to do it, and punish yourself if you don't do it well enough to meet the standards you yourself set. These are the terms on which you work, and they leave little room for self-indulgence, considering the almost universal tendency we have to find our justification in the sheer amount of work we do. Unfortunately, self-sanctioned people are wide open to exploitation. This is because they are frequently treated as though they were being paid for their services. People forget that volunteers work so hard for no financial reward. A gentle reminder is sometimes necessary, and it's a good idea not to wait for resentment to reach too high a pitch before administering it. If you are a volunteer you don't like being taken for granted, and there is no reason at all why you should. The fact is, you may actually be working more productively, at a deeper level of involvement, than when you were paid.

10. Different People, Different Reactions

'Retirement has been an exciting and enriching experience.'
'[My retirement] has been a most interesting and rich experience for my wife and myself and we are enjoying our new "lay" life very much.'
'I got voluntary work with the — Institute, and I enjoyed this so much, I felt much more *useful* than I had in all my years working as a clerk.'
'This period has been a most rewarding one for me and my wife.'
'I retired three years ago from a busy four-parish set-up, but I have found much happiness in the many calls upon me since, and at seventy-three I am busier, if possible, than ever.'
'I feel so lonely. Is this the church I spent my whole life serving?'
'I knew it would be difficult, but I never expected *this*.'

I wrote to the *Church Times* asking for people's experiences of the first five years of retirement. Here are extracts from some of the replies I received. I have divided the replies into three groups: 'trials', 'rewards' and 'surprises'.

Trials
Finding we hadn't managed to get away scot free. The difficulties have taken a couple of years to come home to me. I spent the first year travelling and doing things I wanted to. It was only when I came home again that

I started feeling not being really needed, really wanted
– a feeling of being, well, *bereft*.

Feeling no longer of any worth. If you're reasonably fit and
well, the feeling on retirement is akin to bereavement or
divorce.

Facing up to the inevitable period of sadness. Suddenly
there comes a time when things are no longer there any
more, and it's like a bereavement. A good part of your
life goes when you retire. I'm not afraid to say that I
shed tears. It's nothing to be ashamed of. It's because
you've loved and been loved. And you can't simply
stop, you see. You need a ministry.

Undergoing the abrupt overnight transformation from a
trusted member of the company to someone immediately barred from company premises.

Moving out of a large vicarage into a small bungalow
means you have to let things go that are part of your
married life. It is a time of traumatic changes, don't
underestimate it.

Having to pay positive attention to building up social
relationships instead of enjoying those that came
through working and professional contacts – the lack of
structure deprived me of those periods when I could
enjoy the luxury of a freedom of choice of activity. I had
to learn to overcome guilt feelings about not working.

Not knowing what is going on in the parish and where
things are kept in the church. I long to tidy up the
vestry and silly things like that.

Putting up with people telling you you're making mistakes
about important decisions, such as moving house.

Having to say goodbye to all my pupils.

Having to clear things out of the office where I've worked
for twenty years.

Not having enough room in the new house to have
couples to stay.

Being suddenly someone else. I woke up in the morning
and I hadn't got a job any more. There was no point in
getting up. Why do anything at all?

Having to keep on adjusting, even when you're over the immediate bereavement period.

Thinking of retirement as a time when you're waiting for death, when the main purpose of life is over.

Feeling that you don't want to spend your time entirely in the company of very old people. Sometimes I wonder how many years I have left. I'm quite sure I won't fit in all the things I want to do. Does the church know what to do with us?

Working hard to survive and keep one's head, cool and sane is worth a degree in the humanities! Have you ever wondered why church congregations are 90 per cent (sic) old people?

Keeping an eye open for people who exploit your urge to work and be useful, treating volunteers as if they were a kind of slave labour.

Having to adjust to dealing with an ageing body; slowing down the speed of doing things. I suppose my wife and I had to adjust to having more time together. She said, what do I do with twice as much Colin on half as much pay?

Feeling the occasional sense of guilt at not working as hard as I could.

Having to say goodbye to the most fulfilling career imaginable. My very worst prospect was the farewell party.

Finding that adjusting to early retirement was as close to a concerted campaign to destroy self-esteem as I can imagine.

Rewards

Knowing that the same Lord who guided me through so many years has not left me now, in retirement. I feel really fit and able to continue a fruitful ministry. Routine, learned over the years, has taught me how to organize my freedom, now that I have so much more choice as to what I will do with my time. The sense of freedom is absolutely terrific; I call this my 'third life'.

Being able to see the garden in daylight on winter weekdays; having my wife with me to make up for all those evenings at meetings; being able to postpone jobs until tomorrow; listening to Choral Evensong on Wednesday afternoons.

Being able to enjoy fine weather without having to work; having an opportunity to do things for people at times they can't manage, like shopping for them when places are less crowded.

Coming to realize how happy I felt. We have such joy together and with our family; I felt that I have many things to give to the community and I have the opportunity to do so. Also, I have many more evenings at home.

Watching grandchildren grow up and being useful as a baby sitter. Not being in a flurry or a rush to buy Christmas presents.

Having a chance to lie in sometimes or to sit and watch the sun setting; working in my own time; running my own business, after a lifetime of employed working status; planning changes to take place gradually rather than abruptly; having more time to spend at home with my wife.

Not having to raise money for the diocese or prop up church buildings; being able to 'backtrack' and say no to any work you really don't want to do.

Being able to ride on buses with a free pass, so that I can travel out into the countryside; having respect shown to me as a senior citizen; reading good literature; singing in a choir; going regularly to church; husband and wife, holding hands, sharing the happiness that only age can bring.

Writing pages and pages of letters.

Having time to go and see my friends in hospital; being supportive to people in ways I couldn't be when I was working.

Being free from the incumbent's role to be more myself. This has liberated my preaching and pastoral ministry to individuals and made me available for other kinds of ministry.

Feeling satisfaction, as an early retiree, because my situ-

131

Pastoral ministry is often what goes & is missed th most.

ation was freely chosen. I enjoy the sense of being in charge, of not having to defer to a superior whom one didn't trust or respect on a personal or professional level, of not having to attend tedious and unproductive meetings.

Being free from the hassle: when things go wrong, like the church boiler, or vandals break in, someone else can deal with it and not me. It's good, too, to have time to 'stand and stare', to watch TV and not feel guilty, or have a day out in the car and simply meander around.

Discovering that retirement can be *retyre*ment! What can be better on a summer morning than to drive to a place like Edale and take a service of Holy Communion?

Using the time as a privileged opportunity, with the pressure off, to try to get oneself into better shape for the next chapter of life – I mean death. People who can't cope with the change of tempo at retirement are really missing a very important point.

Having time to talk to anyone and everyone, especially if they need to talk.

Being able to do things I've always wanted to do, but never had time.

Simply enjoying worship without anxiety or responsibility, instead of having to be in charge.

Having so many commitments that I lack the time to focus on some creative interests that I must keep up my sleeve for the future.

Being able to sleep as much as I want, when I want.

Surprises

Experiencing sheer relief and acute disappointment at the same time.

Finding myself swamped by a wave of affection on the day I left.

Discovering how much the staff respected and loved me; the send-off was marvellous and memorable.

Finding love and care in unexpected places; discovering the ability to share with younger people by studying alongside them at the university, where 65+s are welcomed. This was only one of the many surprises the Lord had in store for me when I retired. So many new friends!

Surprising my friends by becoming more domesticated than they imagined possible.

Finding myself getting more easily irritated, less tolerant and even-tempered than I was. There was also great social pressure on me to behave in ways that retired people are expected to, so that I found myself having to contradict fairly forcibly the assumptions which were obvious in comments from acquaintances and relations.

Discovering that families go on in much the same way, and you don't see all that much more of them.

Finding out, after forty years' teaching, how much I really missed contact with kids.

Not having the amount of time to read, listen to music, go walking, that I had expected. When you work from home it's easy to always be doing more, so that I have to discipline myself to take time off.

Discovering that taking a chance (and moving to London) was the best thing we did; and that life could be a lot cheaper because of fare reductions for retired people.

Work flooding in to an extent I had never expected; I have never asked for work, yet am as busy, if not busier, than ever I was when I had four churches.

Finding myself weeping more – usually when singing hymns, but other things trigger it off too.

Finding how tired I was once I stopped work.

Not having the great gap in my life that I had expected to have. What has been surprising is how my time seems to fill itself. It has all been so different from how I expected it to be.

Enjoying so much I never expected. I'm sorry for those who carry on working when they could retire. (Breakfast in bed is easier in a bungalow!)

Finding I like dogs after all. I violently opposed my son's being given one, but I have found our golden retriever very good company.

Getting an insight into what disabled people feel like.

133

Discovering I have to replace clothes less often.

Being amazed that so many years of ministry and parish life could end with so much happiness and so little pain.

Finding out who my friends are – and how little some people I thought of as friends want to know where I'm at.

Finding that my experiences as a teacher are valued, and being invited to lecture in all sorts of places.

Finding that I now have not the slightest wish to be back in the rat race. (This slightly appals me, and I worry about former colleagues, especially those who are workaholics. Are they giving enough time to the non-working side of their lives?)

People made suggestions of a practical bent, involving pensions, insurance, budgeting, and so on. Some of these involve living arrangements and alterations of lifestyle, and concern interests and activities, finding new things to do or reorganizing old routines, so that the time between breakfast and tea may not seem like a life sentence.

On the whole, however, a strong impression is given that the main contribution of the church to pastoral care is both more diffuse and specific than this, lying within the sphere of general emotional support and encouragement. People in the congregation, as well as members of the clergy and church officers, can all take part in a campaign to relieve the psychological pressure on those who are recently retired. This campaign can take weeks or even months. Psychologists who have studied reactions to retirement report responses to the trauma that were still negative after fifteen years. In fact, however, the church as a whole has done more to help retired people rediscover a purpose in life than any other agency. A large proportion of those who 'keep the church going', as PCC members, churchwardens, sidesmen and women, stewards, deacons, elders, and so forth, are retired. So are the Sunday School teachers and the lay readers and preachers, the vergers, sacristans and church caretakers, the lay members of synods and church conferences, not to mention, of course, members of congregations. In fact, the local church is largely a corporation of retired people, presided over by a group of employed people, some of whom have elected to carry on working beyond retirement age.

Because church memberhsip carries with it all sorts of opportunities for involvement in the continuing life of the congregation, retired people frequently find themselves undertaking more work than they can handle, so that they have to back out from jobs simply because they feel that they can't do them as well as they would like. There just aren't enough hours in the day, even though they are retired! In fact, in some cases, they are valuable precisely because they are retired. Committees that meet during the day rather than in the evening use retired people for the running of the church at all levels. This can put considerable strain on those who are no longer as active as they used to be. At the same time, work that is freely undertaken is never so burdensome as work you *have* to do, and the churches benefit from the sheer dedication and enthusiasm of those who give their skills, and their freedom, in this way.

All this is part of a general movement towards a ministry that is genuinely shared, at all levels. Some congregations find openings for retired people, some don't; it still depends very much on the clergy, who are not always as closely in touch with the feelings of the congregation as they might be. This being so, there is a real need for lay intermediaries to bridge the gap.

Norman, for example, has been occupied in a whole range of activities since taking early retirement at sixty. As soon as his vicar, the rural dean, heard of his plans to retire he enlisted him to serve on various deanery committees. One of his less prestigious, but more enjoyable, occupations is to cut the grass of the churchyard with a motor-mower. This is a long job, taking three or four hours. One afternoon, when he was half way through, a stranger came and leaned over the churchyard wall and started to talk to him. Norman knew the man by sight but had never actually spoken to him. The man said that he had also retired, about three months before, in fact. It appeared that he was getting in the way at home; he and his wife were beginning to argue and fall out with each other. This kind of thing never used to happen, he said. He wondered if there was anything he could do in the churchyard – just to keep him out, that was all. Norman was a bit taken aback. He asked the man what sort of work he had in mind. The man said that anything would do; he lived across the road and had his own wheelbarrow and tools. He would walk round the churchyard picking up the rubbish (there was always a good deal of rubbish, thrown over the wall and dispersed by the wind). That, and the bushes needed trimming. In fact there were several small things to be done. He said he wanted a job where he could come and go as he liked. Seeing the state of the churchyard, Norman thought it sounded a good idea and he told the man to carry on.

Several weeks later he saw the man again and had another conversation with him. This time the man, Paul, asked if he could bring a friend with him to help him, as there was more work than he had expected: 'Every time I come, it's just as much of a mess as it was before.' Norman said that he was sure this would be all right. Next week Paul approached Norman again, and asked if he could have a word with him. He had been confirmed when he was fourteen but had never followed it up. He would like to start coming to church again. Would it be all right? He came the following Sunday, bringing his wife and three children with him. After the service Paul told Norman that Dave, who helped him in the churchyard, had spoken about coming to church as well, only his wife was very ill in hospital. Norman told the vicar, who went with him to visit her, taking a bunch of flowers from the churchyard. When, some months later, Dave's wife died, her husband came to church and asked if he, too, might be confirmed like his friend.

As we said in Chapter 1, the total picture tends to be misleading. Many of those who find social support, personal friendship, an outlet for their particular talents, and spiritual comfort and religious self-expression in active church membership would perhaps not have suffered too much from the traumatic aspects of retirement in any event. The feelings that we have been considering in this book do not affect, and afflict, everybody. Some people look forward to retirement very positively, having made definite plans that they can hardly wait to put into operation. Others are delighted at being able to say goodbye to a work situation that has become arduous, or one that has been troubling them for years. Still others are simply very, very tired. Active church members may have been attached to the church for most of their lives in one way or another, and the congregation provides them with precisely that element of continuity and stability that they need at a time like this. All these people have happy memories of having retired and invested themselves even more fully in their beloved church. People who find retirement emotionally disturbing, and turn to the church for some kind of help, are almost certainly in a minority. So how does the church cope with such people?

Not all that well, unfortunately. We have already seen some things that tend to happen when a person suffering from an unresolved life-change turns to her or his local church for help. Instead of immediate emotional support there may be spiritual advice; instead of the provision, or invention, of a social role there is the quiet transfer elsewhere of attention. On a mythological level, one may be urged to behave in ways that are beyond one's reach at such a time. Perhaps most of the failures in helping are really breakdowns of communication; people just don't see that leaving one's job is bound from one point of view or another to constitute a genuine problem. We all *to some extent* cling to the authority we have; continue to identify inappropriately with the role that has been ours for so long; panic when involved in something truly disruptive, reviving our fear about death; feel guilty and lost at not having to turn up for work on Monday morning. Perhaps these things do not all apply at one and the same time to

137

the same person. Perhaps we have been successful in managing to dodge their impact, or to disarm them by our skill in arguing things away – which may unfortunately have the effect of making us less than sympathetic towards those who have not.

I believe that such things are more a matter of the relationship between circumstances than any one factor, be this personal or situational. Retirement happens in as many ways as there are retired people. The event is happy or sad, satisfying or shatteringly painful, according to how it happens, when and where it happens, as well as to whom it happens. In the same way, it is no use saying that retired people should do this or that, because they are all very different. An American psychologist, David Karp, has shown that people's opinions as to the desirability of retirement equate to their current view of their own lives at home and at work. To use the language of psychology, their condition is 'context-specific'. I think that this has been demonstrated in this book.

What one can say, however, is that for some people retirement constitutes a problem; that these people are likely to ask the church for help in some way or another; that Christians as followers of the One who 'went about doing good' are obliged to do what they can for them. What kind of thing, then, can we do? The answer is, first of all and before anything else, we can recognize that they do have a problem. We must not fall into the trap of assuming that just because we have no difficulty with something, everyone else should be able to deal with it as we do – or would do, if it were ours, that is. Secondly, having recognized the presence of a real problem causing real pain, we must not assume that we know the answer, even if we think we do. Hopefully we shall have scrapped at least one 'answer' before the end of our dialogue. The real answer must be the one the retired person arrives at, and this will reflect the particular circumstances affecting him or her much more than it does any course of action that you may think appropriate.

The overall impression given by the letters I received is

one of determined optimism. Many (the majority) have taken the opportunity to say how kind people have been and how grateful they are that they have been fortunate enough to be able to face painful changes in the company of friends. If people complain it is about themselves, their own reactions, rather than about anybody else. They haven't been thankful enough for the kindness and understanding shown to them. The other letters are very different. In fact there is quite a dramatic change of tone from celebration to resentment, with very little in between.

Such a degree of polarization gives rise to some doubts about the letters as a whole. If the majority are so happy and satisfied, how is it that the rest are so very miserable? Sometimes this was because of particularly unfavourable circumstances; usually, however, it appeared to be a case of reacting differently to the same situation. The obvious answer, of course, was that the complainers represented a small minority of people reacting unfavourably to a state of affairs that the majority found quite satisfactory. If this was so then why were the options so limited? Where were the people in the middle? Could it be that the letters revealed a state of affairs in which there was only one acceptable point of view, to which you gave your assent or against which you protested? It really looked as though the majority of people 'agreed too much' because it was unacceptable not to!

After all, these were church people and didn't like to be seen complaining. If they had felt secure enough to be entirely honest with themselves and other people they might not have been so enthusiastic. But even if they were honestly reporting their feelings (and I have no doubt that many of them were) we still have to account for the minority, some of whom definitely needed advice and support. I can't help feeling that if this had been readily available for many of those in the majority, some of these might not have felt themselves constrained to deny any reservations they had about having to pass through a time that cannot, in the nature of things, have been roses *all* the way.

If I were to make one suggestion with regard to all this it would be this: that some kind of counselling system should be set up for those who admit to finding retirement difficult and painful; that it should happen *within* the congregation *for* the congregation; that it should be done in a way that encourages people with private reservations to abandon their public stoicism and share their burdens. In this way the confident ones, enlisted because of their eagerness to help, might find themselves acknowledging their uncertainties while communicating some of their hopes for the future. Each congregation would have to find its own way of doing this, of course.

Counselling, providing jobs with the church organization, helping retired people find voluntary, or in some cases paid, work through local contacts – these are ways in which the church can help retired people. We have already seen how retired people can help the church, the jobs done and positions that they fill within the organization. This is the practical side of their contribution. It bears witness to the wisdom of those who took the trouble to seek out experience and skill where it was to be found and divert it to the church's service. The channelling of so much energy towards the life of the congregation that was formerly directed elsewhere would by itself justify a policy of recruiting church officers and executives among the newly retired.

However, it may be that the greatest benefit is not practical but spiritual – or, rather, practical in its effects but spiritual in origin. It is this: some of the men and women who have passed through the crisis of retirement have discovered faith in God on the way. It is a well-established fact, familiar to every psychologist who studies religious experience, that people find faith at identity crises in their lives. At the crossroads, where the old path fades out, a strange meeting sometimes takes place and life is transformed as a result. At one estimation, over half of all British adults believe that they have had a 'religious or transcendent' experience at least once in their lives. These do not all happen during the crisis of retirement, of course.

On the other hand, we can be reasonably sure that some of them did, and that some churches, wherever they were, benefited from new life of the most invigorating kind. This is the inspirational gift of retired people to the church. It is often confused with the wisdom of experience, which comes from learning how to cope with an increasing number of problems with a growing degree of confidence and skill, a 'more of the same thing' kind of understanding. It is not this, however. This wisdom is the spiritual growth that has come about through the sudden widening of perspectives which happens when one's customary ways of measuring life are removed. Individuation, conversion, inspiration: people call it by various names. The church needs it badly, just as much as it needs youthful enthusiasm and mature common sense.

Finally, it should be pointed out that theology itself can be a source of renewal. At the present time it is leading many retired people into involvement at a deeper level than they have ever known before. Theology has changed and is changing. If you are willing to take another, closer, look you'll find God looking different. There is more growth in theology, more discovery, less received authoritarian pronouncement, fewer stone tablets! Listen to Elizabeth Templeton: 'I have seen people come alive doing theology, so long as they've got away from preconceived ideas of some élitist body of knowledge which they must stuff into their aching bodies and dry souls. Theology for me sets the adrenalin coursing; it has people on mental and physical tiptoe; it stirs things. The only qualification for doing theology is to be alive.' So come on in. For God's sake, don't leave it to the clergy!

alas! They don't
to much.

Appendix 1. Mainly Practical

'People spend more time planning a two-week vacation than planning their retirement,' says Susan Schlipp of the American Organization for Retired Nurses. This is certainly as true in Great Britain as it is in the USA. Ms Schlipp advises those about to retire to 'identify their particular needs and desires' well in advance, and then to find activities that will help achieve them. This exercise should be carried out with a view to the future rather than in terms of the past; those about to retire are urged to write a description of themselves for use two years after retirement without using the words *formerly*, *retired from*, or *husband/wife of*. In a survey of the ideas of older people as to how a successful retirement can be achieved, the Institute of Gerontology at Michigan University found that activities should:

(a) have continuity, so that one can return to them;
(b) be complex and challenging, thus preventing boredom;
(c) fulfil a range of needs and wants;
(d) encourage development and growth;
(e) improve self-esteem;
(f) satisfy the need for accomplishment and creativity.

In other words, retirement activities should fulfil the same needs as work activities, with the exception that you don't get paid for doing them. This is obviously very hard to achieve. The problems surrounding retirement show how hard it is. If this kind of solution were readily available most of the chapters in this book need not have been written. Even the chapter about change could have been toned down quite considerably!

Unfortunately, this is rarely possible. Perhaps it isn't even really desirable. As we saw in Chapter 9, one of the positive things about retirement is that it presents a challenge, part of which involves learning how to enjoy new things in new ways, finding fulfilment in different kinds of roles and relationships. It is not worth sacrificing this in order to live much the same life, be much the same person, as one was before, only poorer. As we have seen, retirement 'opens things out a bit'. If we want to grow, we should take advantage of this. It should not be only because of money that we don't react to life precisely as we used to do, before we retired. From now on our best efforts should go towards exploring the future, not prolonging the past. This is an attitude of mind, a way of looking at life and ourselves, rather than a definite programme of action. In many, even most cases, circumstances prevent our making definite plans for the future. What we can do, however, is work now upon the way we think about what lies ahead of us. What will happen may largely be beyond our control. It is up to us, however, whether we face forwards or backwards.

There are some things we can do to prepare ourselves, of course. Firstly, we can go to courses and seminars about retirement. Large businesses, local authorities, education departments and health authorities, all of which employ large numbers of people, often offer such courses, which are particularly useful for financial information and psychological advice. Such courses differ: the usual subjects offered, however, are information about pensions and benefits, health and fitness, role and attitude changes, and advantages and disadvantages of moving house at retirement. To find out where and when they are held and whether you are eligible to attend, you should contact your local town hall or Citizens' Advice Bureau. These courses tend to devote more time to financial matters than they do to the range of psychological and social issues intrinsically connected with retirement – which is one of my reasons for writing this book. At the same time, our management of money is more important now than it has been for many years. New arrangements have to be made for daily living, including provision for activities associated with a higher proportion of leisure and entertainment than we allowed for when we had less 'free' time.

So far as state retirement benefit goes, 'pensionable age' is 60 for a woman and (currently) 65 for a man. To receive a pension you must, either by yourself ('self-employed') or with your employer, have made National Insurance contributions for 44 (women) or 49 (men) 'qualifying' years. (A qualifying year is one in which you earn at least 52 times the lower earning limit for that year). The number of such years is somewhat less than the number of actual working years. There are four categories of retirement:

A. Basic pension (dependent on number of 'qualifying' years), plus additional pension, dependent on earnings since April 1978.
B. Pensions payable by virtue of another person's earnings and qualifying years. This category applies to married women, widows and widowers.
C. Non-contributory pensions, payable to those who reached pensionable age by 5 July 1948.
D. Non-contributory pensions, payable to those of 80 and over.

The Department of Social Security publish a *Guide to Retirement Pensions* (NP 46, and amendments). Try, if possible, to consult this document, which is available from your local Social Services Department or from offices of the CAB. It has all the information you may need about graduated retirement pensions, invalidity additions, early retirement, working beyond retirement age, income tax, and so on, as well as the implications of having made insufficient contributions or having been out of work because of sickness, unemployment or training. You should also consult a professional person such as a bank manager, accountant or lawyer about your retirement rights and benefits and, if appropriate, about your employer's pension scheme.

If you would like to find an unpaid, but interesting, job to do when you are retired, get in touch with the DVS, the Director of Voluntary Services. Nowadays there is room for voluntary workers in all sorts of areas, in addition to the WVS, who still do so much imaginative and useful work. There are Prison and Hospital Visitors, 'Meals on Wheels', CAB workers, Samaritans, National Trust and English Heritage custodians. Some of these, like Relate (marriage guidance), Samaritans, the CAB, visitors in prisons and hospitals, require special training and aptitude – Samaritans, for instance, is the non-professional profession *par excellence* – and the counselling skills required by Relate may well deter many people, but this may be what you are looking for if you are the kind of person who feels that something has to be difficult to be really worth doing! Some have found their true vocation after retiring from their paid job. Paid or unpaid, these jobs offer you a chance to explore aspects of yourself that have remained undeveloped until now.

Anything that can bring home the importance of retirement and underline the reality of the changes involved is to be recommended. For example, it is a good idea to have a 'family conference' a year or eighteen months before one of you retires, in order to decide on your plan of action with regard to the new state of affairs. This should involve the person, or people, you actually live with before there is any thought of widening its scope to take in other family members and friends. It is obvious that you will need to have some idea as to how you intend to spend your time (and your money!) once you don't have to turn up at work every day of the week. What is not so obvious is the need to plan your activities *together*. If you have been apart during the mornings and afternoons, spending the evening together, you will be used to a pattern of relationship in which you can look forward to seeing each other at certain times. This is extremely important. We need to be apart almost as much as we need to be together. Not wanting to spend every moment of every hour together does not signify an absence of love: as Shakespeare's Feste

145

reminds us, 'Journeys end in lovers *meeting*'. You can't meet someone who is always there! Each couple or group of people needs to plan its own retirement strategy, involving as many meetings and partings as possible, keeping occupied at the same time in order to be free at the same times. This should not be left to chance. Having somebody around all the time can be very tedious if you're not used to it. Once again, this is not a matter of not loving your partner but of keeping your love fresh. It tends to be a rather neglected principle, particularly among church folk, who can interpret it as disloyalty.

Other things need to be talked over as well. Are you going to take the opportunity to move from the district or move to another house or flat in the district? Will a change in the family income make such a move necessary? In ordinary circumstances such a change is almost certain to happen, which is why it is advisable to check on household essentials while you are still working, and have more money than you expect to have at your disposal once you are retired. Washing machines, fridges, vacuum cleaners, cookers may be coming to the end of a long life and need to be replaced while you can afford it. These things should be attended to while you still have a working income. Starting early gives the less domestically skilled partner (usually, but not always, male) a chance to improve his or her ability to play a greater part in running the household when reorganization comes into force.

Most important of all, the person who is to retire should find an opportunity to talk over his or her plans for the future and to make sure that these are understood by, and acceptable to, the person or people he or she will be living with. These pre-retirement months are a time of discussion and experiment, when important elements in our relationships are renegotiated. One thing stands out from the case histories of retirement that I have studied. It is the need for each of us to have some objective in retirement, some positive idea about the kind of things we want to do, the sort of person we want to be during this new stage of our lives. We should not simply shut

146

down, like a train that has reached the end of the line and coasts gently up to the buffers. I have heard stories about people who have died soon after retiring, and I always remember the tendency, noted by Dr Murray Parkes, of bereaved people to die while still comparatively young, following their beloved wives or husbands into an early grave.

Perhaps these 'tragedies of retirement' reflect too great a commitment to a way of life that is no longer available, one entirely taken up with ideas, relationships, routines of work – a life still given over to work, in fact, used up once work was over. 'All he did was watch television until the little white spot came on every night. And eighteen months or so after he retired he passed away. We'd been married for fifty years, but I think it was his job that he was really married to!'

This is the time to make arrangements for paying a visit to your GP for a pre-retirement check-up, and also to review your dietary habits with regard to your future health. Do you really want to go on smoking into your old age? Perhaps you can think of other things to do with your health that could do with attention. What about home safety, for example? Obviously, we need to feel secure against anybody who decides to break in, but how about safety inside the house? What might we trip over if we get out of bed in the middle of the night in order to go to the toilet? Are there lights in the places where you need them? And what about when winter comes – are you going to be warm enough? Retirement is a good time for using your imagination (within reason, that is) and getting down to things before they happen, while you are still active.

There is no doubt that we are all more aware of both the advantages and limitations of being retired nowadays than we were twenty years ago. If death itself was a forbidden subject, retirement seems to have been only rarely written or talked about for its own sake, as an interesting and important human experience, one that it was essential to know about. Rather, it marked the beginning of the grey area of encroaching old age, illness and dependency that would eventually signal the onset of the Unmentionable. The presence of a growing population of retired people who are just as fit, almost as wealthy, and, generally speaking, quite as light-hearted as they ever used to be when they were younger, has largely eroded this particular stereotype, thank God!

Instead, we are beginning to take account of a brand new social phenomenon: a whole section of society with reduced financial responsibility, more leisure time to fill, less restrictive family ties, and in a mood to make the best of life while the opportunity lasts. No wonder that the first people to sit up and take notice are those with something to sell. New situations suggest new ways of making money. Entrepreneurial ingenuity takes many forms. Retirement estates, modelled on the 'retirement towns' of the USA, holiday homes, package tours for the over-sixties, free travel, all bear witness to the commercial respect shown nowadays towards people in their post-retirement years. An advertisement in the local paper invites 'those who are about to retire, or have just retired, or have elderly relatives, parents and friends' along to 'The Retirement Exhibition', to 'make the most of life over 55 by meeting the experts who know how best to help you handle finance, enjoy leisure time, and can give help, advice and ideas about holidays, housing, mobility and legal problems'. The exhibition is organized and sponsored by a long list of local firms interested in selling to the retired.

It is the responsibility of society at large and the Christian Churches in particular to pay attention to what the commercial acumen of other people has revealed. While I have been writing this book I have become more and more aware of the irony of our present situation, in which the wisdom, experience, vitality and imagination of an immense cohort of people is exploited for commercial profit while being ignored so far as almost everything else is concerned. Surely elderly people possess things other than purely commercial potential? The Church has always

148

understood this better than other agencies, continuing to recognize people's abilities and dedication way past retirement age. Perhaps Christians should make more of this fact, in an attempt to redress some of the age prejudice which exists in our society everywhere except in the market-place. We have proclaimed our concern for youth and our protective attitude about families. Could we not now give our considered report about the liveliness and wisdom of age? A Gallup poll conducted some years ago showed that clergy reported that there were only 1 per cent more people aged 65 or above in their congregations than in the parish as a whole. Gallup's comment on this was that 'other surveys reveal that the proportion of over 65s attending a Church of England service is *much greater* than the national population, and from this point of view clergymen considerably underestimated the average age of their congregation'. No doubt they did so because they felt it would 'look better' to overestimate the number of younger people in church. We have been doing this for a long time now. Isn't it time we faced facts, and started to pay attention to a neglected area of very real strength? This is not only strength of numbers, but spiritual strength as well. It has been said, although I don't know by whom, that 'any culture needs the leaven of youthful vigour, experiment, irreverence and drive; but it also needs mature judgement, understanding of and respect for its traditions, otherwise it will be all dazzle and no density'. The fact is that even in the church, judgement and understanding are made to feel isolated and unwanted, especially if the church is the only family they have. They can feel like this even though the work they do may be crucial for the running of the institution. There is no doubt that more should be said and written by the clergy about the contribution made by retired people. We ought not to go on biting the hands that feed us.

Appendix 2. A Retirement Service

Retirement marks an extremely important stage in the lives of many people, bringing with it a second major identity crisis, not so well documented or widely publicized as the adolescent one. As fewer and fewer people are needed to carry out a widening range of work tasks, men and women are likely to find themselves withdrawing from (or being withdrawn from) paid employment at an increasingly early age. In other words, the feeling of loss, of being put on the scrap-heap at the very height of one's powers (having been committed to the job, highly skilled, and free at last from the distractions of establishing a home and building a family) is likely to grow more and more widespread. It is a very disturbing feeling, and many people find that ways of dealing with it, because they depend heavily on the denial of its existence or at least the postponement of acceptance of its real presence, do not prove particularly effective. The feeling seems to be, 'I'm an adult, used to holding down a difficult job with many responsibilities. If I'm old enough to be retired, then I'm definitely old enough to cope with any emotional problems I might have. I don't know what you're talking about, anyway!' But the people close to us do know; and, at a deeper level than the immediately apparent, we know, too. This service attempts to bring these things to the surface of the mind. To this extent, it is an exorcism as well as an initiation, as it aims at integrating within consciousness certain elements which we find unacceptable but which are nevertheless necessary for the restoration of our peace of mind: principally unacknowledged fears

150

concerning the presence of chaos. A service which is intended to symbolize retirement is bound to share at least some of the characteristics of a funeral service. If it does not, it will surely have failed in its object.

All:	*Hymn:* Fill thou my life, O Lord my God (HP 792)
Minister:	May all delightful things be ours, O Lord God: establish firmly all we do.
	The Lord be with you.
All:	And also with you.
Minister:	Lord of our life and governor of all our days, you have given us a time for work and also a time for rest. If we have completed any task successfully, we have done it because of the help you have given us. You have strengthened us in our weakness and supported us when we have failed. Give us grace, Lord, to continue faithfully and courageously in your service until our lives' end, so that we, with all your saints, may live in your eternal presence. Through Jesus Christ. Amen.

The one who is retiring reads from a book which has a definite bearing upon or relevance to his or her job, trade or profession. The minister reads an appropriate biblical passage (e.g. Ecclesiastes 3:1–8 'To every thing there is a season, and a time to every purpose under the heaven').

Minister:	We have come together in God's presence in order to celebrate an event of great personal importance to one of our friends. This is the point in *his* life when *he* must leave behind the joys and sorrows, satisfactions and responsibilities of a way of daily living which *he* has practised for many years, and must now launch out into a new world of experience. We shall try to understand and appreciate how difficult it is to make this voyage into the future, for we are determined that *he* will not have to face the challenge alone. That is

151

why we are accompanying *him* to the threshold of *his* new life. As *he* lays down one set of responsibilities and takes up another, we shall do our best to share those burdens with *him* in accordance with Christ's law. [Philip], you have come to this service in order to receive strength and courage for the present and guidance for the future. Are you willing to go forward into this new stage of your life trusting in God to give you all the things that you need for your journey?

Philip: I am.

Minister: (*to the congregation*) Are you willing to give [Philip] all the help you can, in every way you can?

All: We are.

All: Hymn: Teach me, my God and King (HP 803)
During this hymn, Philip, accompanied by a young representative of his job, trade, profession (perhaps a student or trainee, or someone newly launched on their own career) comes to the front of the congregation. Philip hands over to the young man or woman an implement or an article of clothing associated with the work he has been doing in the past, to be held by them for the rest of the service. Philip then proceeds to the altar and stands silently there for a moment facing away from the congregation, before taking from the altar something that has been placed there to serve as a symbol of his new life; perhaps something that is associated with a skill or an interest to which Philip intends to devote time and effort in the future. Philip moves back towards the congregation, where he is met by a group of friends and/or family members who welcome him into their number. This group now stands in front of the minister.

Group: Father, we ask you to bless [Philip] in *his* new life among us.

Minister: [Philip], the love of the Lord Jesus draw you to himself, the power of the Lord Jesus strengthen you in his service, the joy of the Lord Jesus fill your heart; and the blessing of God Almighty, the Father, the Son and the

Holy Spirit be with you and remain with you always. Amen. (ASB)

The Minister moves forward and shakes Philip's hand and/or embraces him.

All: Hymn: A safe stronghold our God is still. (HP 661)

Minister: In the presence of God, and among his people gathered here, [Philip] has entered on a new stage of *his* journey through life. *He* goes forward from this place confidently and with good courage, for the Lord is with *him* and *his* companions are at his side.

Minister: O Lord God, we commend to you our friend [Philip] as *he* sets out once again on his pilgrimage to you. We thank you for the undiscovered opportunities, joys and challenges that you have in store for *him*. May *he* receive from you wisdom and courage to appreciate without striving, and so grow daily in the knowledge of your love. Through Jesus Christ our Lord. Amen.

All: Our Father . . . deliver us from evil. Amen.

All: Psalm 116.

Minister: The Peace of God which passes all understanding, keep your hearts and minds in the knowledge and love of God, and of his Son, Jesus Christ our Lord; and the Blessing of God Almighty, the Father, the Son and the Holy Spirit, be among you and remain with you always. Amen.

The Lord be with you.

All: And also with you.

Minister: Behold, the whole country lies before you; go wherever you think best.

All: Hymn: God is working his purpose out. (HP 769)

Appendix 3. Community Care Groups

This local Christian initiative is a really creative use of voluntary workers in the service of the community. The majority of those involved have retired from full-time work. I include it as an example of a project that is already functioning, a model of the kind of thing that can happen when people are determined to make use of the very real advantages for service that retirement offers.

A Community Care Group is 'an association of people with various skills who wish to give time to their local community'. It does not limit its service to any one particular category of people, or specialize in any particular field of need. The type of service depends on the need of the neighbourhood, but can include befriending or long-term support, or short-term help in an emergency. Baby- and invalid-sitting, cooking for the elderly sick living alone, shopping and even lawnmowing have all come within the scope of existing care groups. The first of such groups was set up in Hampshire in the 1970s. People interested were told that they should, 'with the help of their incumbent, the Council of Churches, and anyone else who sees the value of a Group, organize a public meeting to sound out local attitudes and discover whether there is sufficient local interest' (Group publicity handout). Three 'golden rules' are laid down for would-be volunteers. These are: that no action must be taken without the explicit permission of the person in need of help; that all information concerning those aided be kept in strict confidence; that help should never be imposed on people, however much assistance might appear to be needed. The stress is always and everywhere upon local action and the neighbourly attitude.

Bee Kenchington, one of those who had the original idea, describes the spread of the movement:

> So often, in times of emergency, people do not know where to turn for help. There are now over forty Community Care Groups operating in the various towns and villages, large and small, in Hampshire. They consist of people who wish to devote some of their time to helping others tackle the ordinary everyday problems that affect us all. The Care Group is a means of sharing the load and providing a resource within the community for meeting needs not being met by any other organization, voluntary or statutory. . . . Care Groups can do a great deal to improve the quality of life for the handicapped, elderly and housebound. In particular, they can become a means of building new relationships within the district and can provide a point of contact for outside agencies needing a local volunteer.

Information about Community Care Groups can be obtained from Bee Kenchington, Flint House, Lordington, Chichester, West Sussex PO18 9DB.

Sources of Further Information

Books

Ronald Blythe, *The View in Winter* (Allen Lane, 1979)

Ivor Brown, *Old and Young* (Bodley Head, 1971)

Willa Cather, *My Antonia* (Virago, 1980)

Alex Comfort, *A Good Age* (Mitchell Beazley, 1977)

Arthur Creber, *New Approaches to Ministry with Old People* (Grove, 1990)

Doris and David Donas, *Young Till We Die* (Hodder & Stoughton, 1973)

Irene Gore, *Age and Vitality* (Unwin, 1979)

Help the Aged, *A Handbook for Retirement: The Time of Your Life* (1979)

Robert Kastenbaum, *Growing Old* (Harper & Row, 1980)

Fred Kemp and Bernard Buttle, *Looking Ahead: A Guide to Retirement* (Continua Productions, 1977)

Una Kroll, *Growing Older* (Collins, 1988)

David Loshak, *Daily Telegraph Guide to Retirement* (Collins, 1978)

Harry Miller, *Countdown to Retirement* (Hutchinson, 1978)

Kate Millett, *Sita* (Virago, 1977)

Myers, Renée, *Retirement: A Guide to Good Living* (Crowood 1990)

Chris Oram, *Going Well over Sixty* (World's Work and *Sunday Times*, 1979)

J.B. Priestley, *Instead of the Trees* (Heinemann, 1977)

—— *Over the Long High Wall* (Heinemann, 1972)

B.F. Skinner and M.E. Vaughan, *How to Enjoy Your Old Age* (SPCK, 1983)

John P. Watts, *Growing Old – Problem or Opportunity?*, Lingdale Paper No 4 (Clinical Theology Association, 1987)

Virginia Woolf, *Diaries* (Hogarth Press, 1987–8)

Periodicals

Choice Monthly magazine published for the Pre-Retirement Association, Bedford Chambers, Covent Garden, London WC2 8HA

New Age Quarterly magazine of Age Concern, Bernard Sunley House, 60 Pitcairn Road, Mitcham, Surrey CR4 3LL

Old Age Annual register of social research, published by the Centre for Policy on Ageing, Nuffield Lodge, Regent's Park, London NW1 4RS

Yours Monthly newspaper for the elderly, available from PO Box 126, Watford WD1 2HG

Organizations

Age Concern, Bernard Sunley House, 60 Pitcairn Road, Mitcham, Surrey CR4 3LL

Age Resource, 1268 London Road, London SW16 4EJ (Local projects and opportunities)

British Association of Retired Persons, 14 Frederick Street, Edinburgh EH2 2HB

British Pensioners and Trade Union Action Committee, c/o Islington Task Force, 10 Corsica Street, London N5

Centre for Policy on Ageing (formerly the National Corporation for the Care of Old People), Nuffield Lodge, Regent's Park, London NW1 4RS

CRUSE (National Organization for Widows and their Children) 126 Sheen Road, Richmond, Surrey TW9 1UR

Employment Fellowship, Drayton House, Gordon Street, London WC1H 0BE

Galleon World Travel Association, Galleon House, King Street, Maidstone, Kent ME14 1EG

Help the Aged, 32 Dover Street, London W1A 2AP

Holiday Fellowship, 142–4 Great North Way, London NW4 1EG

Link Opportunity, Bernard Sunley House, 60 Pitcairn Road, Mitcham, Surrey CR4 3LL

National Benevolent Fund for the Aged, 65 London Wall, London EC2M 5TU

National Council for the Single Woman and Her Dependents, 29 Chilworth Mews, London W2 3RG

National Federation of Housing Societies, 30–53 Southampton Street, London WC2 7HE

Over-Forty Association for Women Workers, Mary George House, 120–2 Cromwell Road, London SW7 4HA

Pensioners' Voice (National Federation of Old Age Pensioners' Associations) 91 Preston New Road, Blackburn, Lancs BB2 6BD

Pensions Campaign Centre, Transport and General Workers Union, 16 Swains Lane, London N6 6QS

Pre-Retirement Association, 19 Undine Street, London SW17 8PP

Public Appointments Unit, Civil Service Department, Whitehall, London SW1

REACH (Retired Executives Action Clearing House), 1st Floor, Victoria House, Southampton Row, London WC1B 4DH

Relate, Herbert Gray College, Little Church Street, Rugby CV21 3AP

Right to Fuel Campaign, 7 Exton Street, London SE1 8UE

Saga (Senior Citizens) Holidays Ltd, 119 Sandgate Road, Folkestone, Kent CT20 2BN

Samaritans, 10 The Grove, Slough SO1 1QP

Success after Sixty, 14 Great Castle Street, London W1N 8JU

University of the Third Age, 1 Stockwell Green, London SW9 9JI

Workers' Educational Association, Temple House, 9 Upper Berkeley Street, London W1H 8BY

Bibliography

Introduction

Age Concern, 'Profiles of the elderly', *Age Concern Research Publications*, Vol. I, Mitcham, Surrey

Falkingham, J., 'Dependency and aging in Britain: a re-examination of the evidence', *Journal of Social Policy*, XVIII(2), 1989: 211–33

Phillipson, P., 'Towards a sociology of retirement', *Reviewing Sociology* (New Series), 6(2), 1989: 3–9

Chapter 1

de Bono, E., *Lateral Thinking* (Penguin, 1970)

Bromley, D.B., *The Psychology of Human Aging* (Penguin, 1966)

Festinger, L., *A Theory of Cognitive Dissonance* (Stanford University Press, 1957)

Kelly, G., *A Theory of Personality* (Norton, 1963)

Perls, F.S., Hefferline, R.F. and Goodman, P., *Gestalt Therapy* (Penguin, 1973)

Chapter 2

Barrie, J.M., 'Peter Pan', *Collected Plays* (Hodder & Stoughton, 1928)

Janov, A., *The Primal Scream* (Putnams, 1970)

Karp, D., 'The social construction of retirement among professionals 50–60 years old', *The Gerontologist*, 29, 6, 1989: 750–9

Kaufman, J.E., 'Leisure and anxiety: a study of retirees', *Activities, Adaptation and Aging*, II, I, 1988: 1–10

Lake, F., in M. Yeomans (ed.) *Clinical Theology* (Darton, Longman & Todd, 1988)

Rank, O., *Beyond Psychology* (Dover, 1958)

Salvendy, J., 'Brief psychotherapy at retirement, *Group*, 13, I, 1989: 43–57

Tournier, P., *Guilt and Grace* (Hodder & Stoughton, 1962)

Chapter 3

Berger, P. and Luckmann, T., *The Social Construction of Reality* (Penguin, 1966)

Bettelheim, B., *The Informed Heart* (Penguin, 1986)

Bullock, A. and Stallybrass, O., *The Fontana Dictionary of Modern Thought* (Collins, 1977)

Rank, O., *Beyond Psychology* (Dover, 1958)

Storr, A., *The Integrity of the Personality* (Penguin, 1963)

Chapter 4

Bowlby, J., *Attachment and Loss* (Penguin, 1981, 3 vols)

Gorer, G., *Death, Grief and Mourning in Contemporary Britain* (Cresset, 1965)

Grainger, R., *The Unburied* (Churchman, 1988)

Hobson, R., 'My Own Death' *New Blackfriars*, Oct. 1970

Kelly, G., *A Theory of Personality* (Norton, 1963)

Kubler-Ross, E., *On Death and Dying* (Tavistock, 1970)

Lambourne, R.A., in M. Wilson (ed.), *Explorations in Health and Salvation* (Birmingham University, 1983)

Parkes, C.M., *Bereavement: Studies of Grief in Adult Life* (Tavistock, 1972)

Roebuck, J., 'When does old age begin? The evolution of the English definition', *Journal of Social History*, 12, 1979: 416–28

Speck, P., *Loss and Grief in Medicine* (Baillière Tindall, 1978)

Weber, M., *Sociology of Religion* (Methuen, 1965)

Chapter 5

Bannister, D. and Fransella, F., *Inquiring Man* (Croom Helm, 1986)

Goffman, E., *The Presentation of Self in Everyday Life* (Penguin, 1971)

Hillman, J., *Healing Fiction* (Station Hill, 1983)

Kelly, G., op. cit.

Mead, G.H., *Mind, Self and Society* (University of Chicago Press, 1967)

Ratna, L., 'Two kinds of psychosocial crisis that retirement can provoke', *Geriatric Medicine*, Feb. 1987

Chapter 6
Anderson, O., Antonovsky, A. and Sagy, S., 'Family, gender, and attitudes towards retirement', *Sex Roles*, 20, 7/8, 1989: 355–69
Cox, H., *The Secular City* (SCM, 1965)
Erickson, E., *Childhood and Society* (Penguin, 1965)
Foucault, M., *Madness and Society* (Tavistock, 1967)
Marcuse, H., *Eros and Civilisation* (Sphere, 1969)
Ratna, L., op. cit.
Richardson, A. (ed.), *A Theological Word-Book of the Bible* (SCM, 1950)
Tawney, R.M., *Religion and the Rise of Capitalism* (Penguin, 1984)
Weber, M., op. cit.

Chapter 7
Jacobi, J., *The Psychology of C.G. Jung* (Routledge, 1962)

Chapter 8
Jacobi, J., op. cit.
Mulkay, M. and Ernst, J., 'The changing profile of social death', *Arch. Europ. Sociol.* XXXII, 1991: 172–96
Watts, J.P., 'Growing Old: Problem or Opportunity?, *Lingdale Paper No. 4* (Clinical Theology Association, 1987)

Chapter 9
Bovet, T., *Have Time, Be Free* (SPCK, 1968)
Fordham, F., *An Introduction to Jung's Psychology* (Penguin, 1953)
Kelly, G., op. cit.
McGuire, W. and Hull, R.E.C. (eds), *C.G. Jung Speaking* (Thames and Hudson, 1978)

Chapter 10
Karp, D., 'The social construction of retirement among professionals 50–60 years old', *The Gerontologist*, 29, 6, 1989: 750–9

Appendix 1
Schlipp, S., 'Plan now to make your retirement active and productive', *AORN Journal* (American Association of Retired Nurses), 50, 6, 1989